C000075908

Just Jill

The Autobiography of Jill Allen-King OBE

Just Jill

The Autobiography of Jill Allen-King OBE

Jill Allen-King OBE

Foreword by Lord Colin Low CBE

APEX PUBLISHING LTD

Hardback first published in 2010, Updated and Reprinted in 2010.
Printed in paperback in 2016 by

Apex Publishing Ltd

12A St. John's Road, Clacton on Sea, Essex, CO15 4BP, United Kingdom
www.apexpublishing.co.uk

Copyright © 2010-2016 by Jill Allen-King OBE
The author has asserted her moral rights

British Library Cataloguing-in-Publication Data
A catalogue record for this book
is available from the British Library

ISBN: 978-1-78538-497-4

All rights reserved. This book is sold subject to the condition, that no part of this book is to be reproduced, in any shape or form. Or by way of trade, stored in a retrieval system or transmitted in any form or by any means, electronic, mechanical, photocopying, recording, be lent, re-sold, hired out or otherwise circulated in any form of binding or cover other than that in which it is published and without a similar condition, including this condition being imposed on the subsequent purchaser, without prior permission of the copyright holder.

Typeset in 10.5pt Arial

Production Manager: Chris Cowlin

Cover Design: Siobhan Smith

ACKNOWLEDGEMENTS

I would like to thank Apex Publishing for giving me the opportunity to publish my life story. I would also like to thank my daughter, Jacqueline, who helped me to transcribe the book over the first few years of writing it. Finally, my thanks go to Peter Wilkins, who has taught me how to use a computer, which has been a useful tool for completing this book. Peter, being a secretary and proofreader. Thanks also to Moira McConnell, who has helped me with other aspects of this work, and Betty Harper, who helped sort and select the photographs.

CONTENTS

FOREWORD

This is a remarkable book by a remarkable person who has led a remarkable life.

Jill Allen-King's life has certainly not been short on incident or drama. She had to have one eye removed on account of measles on her first birthday. When she was 13, her aunt and uncle were drowned in the Canvey Island floods of 1953 and Jill was drafted in to help with the clean-up. Having been told to conceal her visual impairment, school was a struggle for want of the appropriate support. Nevertheless, Jill acquitted herself well and went on to college to study catering and then securing work as a cook for Shell and then the directors of Gallaher's, the cigarette manufacturers, in the City of London. She was active in the Girls' Life Brigade and was also a keen dancer.

However, at the age of 24, all this came to an abrupt halt when Jill's sight went completely on, of all days, her wedding day. Health and Social Services failed her badly, providing nothing in the way of information or support. What little advice they did give was just plain wrong; for instance, that her eye condition made it necessary for her to be sterilised after the birth of her daughter so that she had no more children. This was simply medical prejudice that a blind person could not or should not bring up children. As a result, Jill found herself with little in the way of help, newly married, soon to have a young child, unable to go out by herself and believing that the active life she had previously enjoyed was at an end.

Fortunately, Jill had too much spirit to remain in this condition for long. Gradually, over the first few years, she resumed her knitting, her dancing and her dressmaking. She was asked to take charge of a Girls' Life Brigade company again. She received mobility training and acquired her first guide dog. Through meeting other blind people she began to learn what non-sighted people can do, gained the confidence to put it into practice for herself and then spread the word to others. Newspaper, radio and television reporters began to take an interest and the rest, as they say, is history.

Over the years she has made literally hundreds of broadcasts and given hundreds of talks to schools and church groups, etc., and she has raised thousands of pounds for charity. Above all, she has been a leading member of organisations for the blind and disabled, determined to defend the interests of blind people and secure their rights at local, national and international level. She has been particularly associated with campaigns for access to transport and the built environment, to make our streets and pavements safe for pedestrians to walk on and to ensure that household goods are manufactured according to 'design for all' principles, so that everyone can use them. But she hasn't just confined herself to the concerns of the blind and disabled. She is active within the Liberal Democrat Party and has twice stood for the Council, narrowly missing election.

What is the secret of her success? She is tenacious and determined. As this book demonstrates, she is a veritable human dynamo and completely indefatigable. She has a very good memory, great skill in mobilising and deploying arguments and a graphic way of putting things that is easy for people to grasp and difficult for them to forget. As she says, people don't readily forget her. She can engage the attention of the Queen and Princess Diana for minutes at a stretch. She is on familiar terms with Ministers, and when she shakes them by the hand she does not let go until she has finished with them. And the little band of helpers she has organised testifies to the loyalty she inspires.

This is a story that deserves to be read. It will serve as an inspiration to the many thousands of people each year who find themselves suddenly without sight and at a loss what to do, and as an education to the many millions of sighted people who lack a proper appreciation of what the blind can do and need. It also contains many useful tips on how to manage as a blind person, and could serve as a little bible for campaigners who would follow in her footsteps. But the good news for everyone is: Jill is still only 70 and is still going strong.

Lord Colin Low CBE

INTRODUCTION

When I was born in 1940 my parents had no idea of the shocks and surprises I was to give them: losing the sight in my right eye through measles on my first birthday and going totally blind on my wedding day as a result of glaucoma at the age of 24, followed by the birth of my daughter Jacqueline.

In 1983 I was awarded the MBE for campaigning to gain access for guide dogs and for initiating tactile paving at pedestrian crossings. I had appeared in many local and national newspapers and on local and national radio and television. I divorced Mick, who was sighted, and married Alvin, a blind man.

My parents have now died and, having spent over 46 years totally blind but leading a very busy and active life, before I lose all my memories I must spend time writing them all down.

I did start to write my life story in 1988 when Jacqueline had just left home to get married, but my mother was taken ill with the flu, which led to a leg amputation and eventually her death. I was still busy with my campaigning work, so I had no time for writing, but let's hope that this time I will be more successful. I said in 1988 that God would help me to find the time, as he had guided me through my life, but then was obviously not the right time.

It is now August 2009. I live with my husband Alvin, who is 67, and my sixth guide dog, Amanda, who is now five years old. My grandchildren, Joseph aged 16 and Emily aged 13, live with their parents, Jacqueline and Michael, in Hampshire.

Following the death of my Uncle Bernard in 2000, with the money he left me I was eventually able to buy my first computer, which has enabled me to complete this book.

CHAPTER 1 – MY CHILDHOOD

My grandparents, Pauline and Alfred Griffith, lived at 112, Southbury Road, Enfield, Middlesex. They were first cousins when they were married. They had three children, the first being my father, Alfred, born in 1910, followed by Connie and Bernard, born three years apart. My grandparents had a holiday home on Canvey Island in Essex, which was called 'Dickies Nook', and I can remember many happy holidays there. To reach Canvey you travel through Benfleet, so when my parents were looking for somewhere to live when they married in 1937 they had become acquainted with that area and bought a two-bedroom bungalow in Philmead Road, Benfleet, where they lived until 1952 before moving to Southview Road.

My mother, Maudie Clarke, had lived in Ponders End with her aunt and uncle, Maud and Sid Jefferies, who had brought her up following the death of her mother when she was only 12 years old. Her mother, Miriam, had spent her final seven years in a mental hospital, having suffered a breakdown following the loss of her husband in 1917 during the First World War. His name, Stanley Able Clarke, is on the Cenotaph in Golders Green in London. In those days there was no treatment for psychiatric illnesses, and my mother never got over not having a mother and father to bring her up.

Mum was only 15 when she met my dad, who was 18. He looked after her and eventually married her when she was 22, the ceremony taking place at Enfield Methodist Church on 18th September 1937. I was already on the way when war broke out in 1939 and my dad joined the army.

It was snowing heavily when my mother went into labour and had to travel by bus to Southend Hospital, where I was born on 10 March 1940. I was actually due to make my arrival on 1st March, St David's Day, and my mum and dad had been hoping for a son, whom they intended to call David. So when I arrived ten days late and was female they were very disappointed, and

1

my mum would remind me of this throughout my life. My response was to tell her how much I wanted a brother or a sister.

I was born a fit and healthy baby and my mother breastfed me for many months. As the war continued to rage, my grandparents insisted that my mother should take me to live with them in Enfield. My mother did not want to go and all her life she resented the fact that she was made to take me there, the place where all my troubles started.

My mum was persuaded, very reluctantly, to take me to the clinic. Just before my first birthday I was not well and my grandma wanted to call the doctor, but my mother said there was nothing wrong with me. On the day of my birthday other members of my family could see that I was very ill - I could not see to blow out the candle on my cake. I only found out what really happened on that day when my own daughter was three years old and we visited my grandma's sister, Auntie Doris, who lived in Shaldon in Devon. She told me what had really happened at that time, but she made me promise never to let my mother know that I knew the truth.

My grandma, who had a heart condition, had to fake a heart attack so that they could get a doctor into the house to look at me. The doctor diagnosed measles and bronchial pneumonia and I was rushed into Chase Farm Hospital. From there I was transferred to Moorfields Eye Hospital, where I had to have my left eye removed.

My dad was brought home on compassionate grounds and, in addition to the trauma of continual German bombing raids, my parents had to cope with the shock of my becoming blind in one eye. Although my mother must have known that it was her fault for not getting the doctor to see me earlier, she always tried to treat me as though I had no disability. I always wore glasses and had a good artificial eye, so no one could tell that I was blind in one eye. My dad had a different attitude to the situation. He was very fond of me and was extremely upset about my condition.

I am not sure how long it was before we returned to Benfleet, but the war was still on. At the end of the war my father took up his job again with the Cooperative Wholesale Society selling ladies' shoes. He travelled every day from Benfleet to Fenchurch

Street station until he retired through ill health in 1967. My father longed to have another child, but my mother said she had enough work on her hands coping with me. I also would have loved a brother or sister, not only when I was a child but also in difficult times such as when my parents died, which I found very hard to deal with alone.

Our bungalow in Benfleet was very small, but it had a very large garden. We had lots of lovely fruit trees, so we always had fresh plums, apples and pears. My dad also had an allotment where he grew vegetables. Even as a very little girl I loved scented flowers, and I can remember a beautiful lavender bush that grew near our gate.

The war raged until I was six years old, and I can remember the air-raid shelter in our back garden where we hid every time the sirens went off, together with our black cat, Blackie, and our golden spaniel, Sally. When my dad returned from the war in 1947 we had some chickens and had fresh eggs every day.

We were very poor and so I did not have many toys. I longed for a doll's pram when I was little, but my dream did not come true until I was ten years old, by which time I was really too old to play with a pram. However, my parents did buy me a tricycle, and when I was ten years old I was given a second-hand two-wheeler, which I was thrilled to bits with. I would often use it for shopping errands for my mother and lots of other people. However, I never rode my bicycle on the pavement, as I knew that the local policeman would tell me off.

When the time came for me to go to school, the doctor at Moorfields advised my mother that I should attend a small school rather than the large school at Benfleet, so I was sent to St Margaret's Church of England School at Bowers Gifford, which meant a journey of about half an hour involving two bus rides. My mother told me never to tell anyone that I was blind in one eye, although my condition put quite a strain on me. I struggled with my school work, as I could not always see what was written on the blackboard and had problems reading the small print in books, and I was always very unhappy every morning when my mother left me at the school.

Despite the difficulties of being at an ordinary school without any special help for me as a partially sighted child, I was pleased that I had not been sent away to a special school. Although I probably would have learnt a lot more academically, I would have been away from my family for most of the year and would have missed growing up in my local community. If Low Vision Aids had been made available to me I know that I would have learnt much more than I did, and I was very upset when I did not pass the scholarship.

Fortunately the St Margaret's school building was single storey and quite small, and each classroom door was a different colour, which made it easy for me to get around. I can remember there was a long step in front of the doorway that had a white line running along the edge, which stopped me from falling up and down it, and my first teacher, Miss Balham, allowed me to sit at the front of the class.

I lived too far away to go home at lunchtime, so I always had a hot cooked dinner at school, which I loved – so much so that I would try to get second helpings. The cook was called Mrs Mitchell, and I would go and stand at the kitchen door and watch her preparing the dinners. This was how I became interested in the catering profession. One of my mother's aunts had been a cook at Lyons Corner House, so I suppose it was in my blood. In my last year at school I was the dinner monitor and served lunches to the teachers. I can remember being given a book as a prize at the end of term for doing this and I was so thrilled.

As it was a church school we had a little chapel in the grounds, and every morning we had a short service there. I quickly learnt the hymns by heart and I loved that time of day. On special occasions in the church calendar we would all walk to St Margaret's Church, located about half a mile from the school. It was, and I am sure still is, a lovely old-fashioned church situated next to the railway line. I still travel on that train route regularly and I often think of those happy days at that church. In the summer we would often walk home, going past the church and following the rail track until we reached our bungalow, which was only a few hundred yards from the railway line. In fact my father's allotment backed onto the railway and I can remember sitting on a little bench there watching the steam trains go by. I never dreamt that I would travel on those trains as much as I have done and still do.

Friends have meant a lot to me during my life, and the first friend I can remember was Adrian Eatwell, who lived next door to me. He had red hair and used to sit on the top of the fence to talk to me. He attended a private school and lived with his mother and grandmother. I could never understand why he had no father. David Cowan, the son of one of my mother's close friends, travelled to school with me, and at the bus stop we would meet Barbara Taylor, who remained my friend for many years. Another girl who looked after me at school was Norma Hillier. She was head girl and I was very sorry when she left to go to another school.

The headmistress at Bowers Gifford School was called Miss Ashton, but we all had to call her 'madam'. She was very strict but she was very kind to me with my sight problem. When I was six years old I was taught how to knit and sew, and although I was not very skilled at that time due to my poor vision I did remember what I had been taught and made good use of that instruction when I eventually went totally blind.

I learnt to read and write with my limited sight but chose more physical activities rather than reading, although we did go every week to the local library in Benfleet. I used to love looking at the royal family picture books, and again I never dreamt that one day I would meet so many members of the royal family, let alone go to Buckingham Palace on several occasions.

The first time I can ever remember being on a stage was when I was about four or five. It was 1944, when my mum was a member of the local Women's Institute and the wives of the men that were away serving in the war used St Mary's Hall, Benfleet, for their meetings. They decided to put on a show and chose The Wizard of Oz. I was dressed up as a robin and had to do a little dance. At that time I was already going to Santoy School of Dancing, as dancing was my favourite hobby, and it has given me much pleasure all my life. I studied tap and ballet from the age of about two, and I also had ballet classes with Miss Blelock in Leigh, not far from where I live now, when I was seven years old. I passed all my Royal Academy of Dancing exams and I am thrilled that my granddaughter, Emily, also went to ballet and still goes to dancing lessons. I started ballroom and Latin American dancing when I was 18 years old, but more about that later. I was also 18 when I had my first experience of using a microphone to speak to a crowd of people. My mum and I had gone to a holiday camp in St Austell Bay, Cornwall. I cannot remember if my dad was with us, but I think he might have been at a Scout camp. There was a personality competition and I won it, so I became Miss Duporth and it was my job to compère the week's activities. I also entered the fancy dress competition with two friends I had made there, and we went as the Butcher, the Baker and the Candlestick Maker. I cannot remember how well we did, but it was all good fun.

As well as dancing, music also played a big part in my family's life. My grandfather, great-grandfather and great-great-great-grandfather all worked for Boosey & Hawkes, the music company, making musical instruments and also playing them in the Enfield Brass Band. My mother could play the piano well, and I started to learn it too when I was about eight, but after a year I gave it up because I could not see the music. I kept the piano after losing my sight, in the hope that I could still be taught to play, but my first social worker for the blind said that this would not be possible unless I learnt Braille music. As I had only been blind for a couple of years at that point and was still coming to terms with my disability, I did not want to learn Braille, so my husband took my piano to the dump at Leigh Tip. I was very upset and have always regretted this. Music continues to run in the family. My daughter learnt to play the trumpet and was in the 1st Southend Girls' Brigade band, who were the national champions for a number of years. In 1977, the Queen's Silver Jubilee year, their band led the youth parade up The Mall, and they also appeared on Blue Peter and played in Southend carnival and at many fêtes. My granddaughter, Emily, has been learning to play the saxophone at school, and my husband runs a music shop, but I'll tell you more about that later.

My dad had been a member of the Cub Scouts in Enfield, and when he got married and moved to Benfleet he started attending Benfleet Methodist Church and became a Scout master. He was dedicated to the Scouts and worked with them until he died. Again, it gives me great pleasure to know that my grandson Joseph was a Cub where he lives in Hampshire. My mother started to help in the Sunday school, playing the organ, so I naturally went to the Sunday school, which was run by Mr Downer. His son John was in my class and I still see him from time to time now.

I joined the Brownies when I was seven and stayed until I was ten years old, when my mother was asked by the minister, Rev John Stacey, if she would go to the Thundersley Methodist Church to help run a Girls' Life Brigade (GLB) company. This she did and I went with her to that church. My dad was never happy that I had left the Benfleet church and that I did not attend the Guides. My mother became captain of the company and by 1953 had over a hundred girls. I used to help by taking the young cadets.

After leaving my primary school I transferred to the local secondary school, called Shipwrights, which recently has changed its name to King John. This was a very large school with over a thousand pupils. I probably should have gone to a special school at that time, but no one said anything so I carried on as best I could. I took part in all the school activities, and considering my lack of vision I did quite well, managing to be in the top stream for maths and English. My cookery teacher was Miss Riley, whom I can remember well. She had black hair, wore bright red lipstick and dressed in a spotless white overall. It was Miss Riley who taught me how to iron properly, which at the time I thought was a waste of time. However, when I became totally blind and needed to iron all my husband's shirts I remembered those lessons well, because when you are blind you have to work systematically. I managed to get into the school netball and hockey teams, but my lack of vision stopped me from getting many goals. Mrs Punt was my needlework teacher and she taught me very well how to sew by hand and machine, but I really was not very good. However, what she taught me stood me in good stead for the years ahead when sewing would mean so much in my life.

I had many friends at school but sadly have lost contact with

7

them all now. My two best friends were Roberta Heyward and Anne Coleman. In the GLB Peggy Law was my best friend, but she attended a different school. Another friend was Jacqueline Doubleday, and she was the reason I named my daughter Jacqueline.

In 1951 I went on my first camp with the GLB to Kessingland and had a good time. Other years we went to Teignmouth in Devon and stayed at St Michael's Church Hall. My grandmother's sister and her husband lived in Teignmouth and so we had been there for holidays when I was younger. I can still remember the Devon views.

The year 1953 was a year I would never forget. It started with the Canvey Island floods, in which my aunt and uncle were drowned. They had retired to Canvey from Mill Hill, buying a bungalow next door to my grandparents' bungalow in Newlands Road, which was very close to where the sea wall broke. Aunt Edie was one of my grandfather's sisters. Uncle Bernard and my dad had gone out in a boat to try to rescue them, but the water had reached the ceiling of their home. Fortunately my grandma and granddad were not down for the weekend from Enfield. A local reporter came to our bungalow to telephone the story of the floods through to the national press.

As my school was used to accommodate people whose homes had been flooded, we had three weeks off school. One of my dad's friends worked for Hawkins Electrics and provided washing machines in the Benfleet school, where we helped to do the flood washing. It was while we were there that we met the Queen Mother, who was visiting all the flood areas. After the floods subsided we took the washing machines over to Canvey and did the washing in the British Legion Hall. I actually spent my thirteenth birthday there and can remember my grandma and Uncle Bernard bringing me a clock as my birthday present. Although Uncle Bernard lived on Canvey until he died in 2000 and I would visit him there many times, I would never sleep there after the floods.

It was only a short time after that when I had an accident on my bicycle; in fact it was the Thursday before Easter. I was riding along Clifton Avenue, a road just near where I lived, when I heard

8

a noise to my right. As a plane had crashed earlier in the year, I was worried that the noise might be another plane coming down. I turned my head to the right and did not see the stationary lorry on the left, my blind side, so I crashed into it. A neighbour took me home and my parents called an ambulance. I was taken to Southend Hospital, where I had three stitches in my lip, and I had also lost a front tooth. Apart from the injuries to my mouth I was not too badly hurt, but I still had to have three weeks off school, most of it falling within the Easter holidays. I went to stay with my grandma in Enfield and I can remember one day Uncle Bernard took us for a ride into the Kent countryside. We went to a café for lunch and had steak and kidney pudding. We never forgot that meal. Uncle Bernard would always call food 'lovely grub', much to the annoyance of my grandma, but she always ended up laughing, as she knew we loved our food. She was a good cook as well and I used to love to stay with her. I was very embarrassed when I went back to school without my front tooth, as it took three weeks for the false one to be made.

My mother ran the GLB company until 1955, when her doctor advised her to give it up as she was doing too much and was on the verge of a nervous breakdown. Two of the officers in the GLB at Crowstone Congregational Church in Westcliff were friends she had worked with as dinner ladies at a local school, and so she went there and just played the piano for them. At this time in my life I was just leaving my secondary school and had decided to go to Southend Municipal College to do a Hotel and Catering course. I was only 15, but I was already quite grown up, largely due to the experience I'd had the previous summer in Guernsey.

In the summer of 1954 I had gone on holiday with my dad and friend Peggy Law to Guernsey for two weeks. My mum did not come with us as she had gone on a camping holiday with the GLB and did not want to travel by boat. We travelled by train to Southampton and then boarded the overnight boat to Guernsey. As we embarked on our 12-hour journey a violent storm started, and all night long I was really seasick. We stayed in the Rosedale Guest House run by a Mr and Mrs Bennett. Mr Bennett was a tailor in St Peter Port while his wife ran the guesthouse.

On arrival I was still ill from the stormy boat ride and stayed in bed for three days. I dreaded the journey home, and so after a talk with Mrs Bennett it was suggested that I should stay on for two weeks and help her in the guesthouse. She knew I was going into the hotel and catering profession and thought that the experience would do me good. She also offered to pay for me to travel home by plane, which was like a dream come true, as I could not face the boat trip back again. My dad telephoned my mum to make sure that she agreed, as I was still at school and quite young. She left it up to my dad to decide and I am so pleased that he allowed me to stay.

I can remember so well standing at St Peter Port harbour waving goodbye to my dad and my friend Peggy. For the first time in my life I felt very alone, but at the same time I was relieved not to be making that boat journey.

I really enjoyed my two weeks helping to serve meals to the guests and making beds. I also assisted in the kitchen. Every afternoon was spent walking to the lovely local beaches in the hot sunshine, and I can still visualise the colours of the sea and the scenery of Guernsey. When the time came for me to fly home I was feeling quite grown up. Mr Bennett had made me a slim grey pencil skirt to wear and my dad had sent me a pair of red sandals with a little heel. This was the first pair of shoes I had ever owned with a platform heel. I travelled to Northolt airport, and when my mum and dad met me they could see I had changed from a schoolgirl into a young woman.

I returned to Guernsey the following year, working for nine weeks at the guesthouse during my college recess. Once again, Mrs Bennett paid my Heathrow/Guernsey airfare, which cost 11 pounds return. In addition to full board and accommodation, I earned 30 shillings a week. I worked very hard, learnt a lot and enjoyed every minute of the experience.

CHAPTER 2 – ENTERING THE BIG, WIDE WORLD

In 1955 I was 15 years old and began my two-year Hotel and Catering course at Southend Municipal College. I also started to go to Crowstone Church and joined the 2nd Westcliff Company of the GLB, where my mum had gone to play the piano. I had seen many of the girls there at my college, although not in the same department. The college was situated at Victoria Circus, in the middle of Southend, and I took the train from Benfleet Station. On my first day I was waiting for the train when a girl came up to me and asked me if the train went to Southend. After replying we made friends and I have been friends with her ever since. Her name was Marion Hughes and she lived on Canvey Island. She was attending a secretarial course at the college, and after leaving college we often travelled on the train together when we both worked in London.

I had only been at college a few days when I met my first boyfriend, Peter Sawkins. We started to go out together and our first kiss was at the college dance, which was held at the Queens Hotel in Hamlet Court Road in Westcliff. I can remember my dad bought me a beautiful strapless lavender dress with a little matching bolero covered with rosebuds. Unfortunately Peter could not dance and never did learn, but he was a member of the Thames Estuary sailing club, and although I could not swim I went sailing every week in the summer off the beach at Westcliff. In the winter we would go to Brandy Hole. I always wore a life jacket but luckily we never capsized. We also went to the pictures every week, usually at the Odeon Cinema. Peter's parents were very kind to me and treated me as if I was their daughter. They had two sons, Peter and David, but their first child, a girl, had died. Even when Peter and I split up three years later, they still kept in touch with me right up until 1983, when I believe Mrs Sawkins died; in fact, my present husband still has Mrs Sawkins' phone number. Peter left college before me as he failed his exam, and he went to work in a hotel in Haywards Heath. Every weekend I would travel to London, meet him at Victoria Station and travel by bus to Liverpool Street Station. This was because Peter lived at Thorpe Bay at the time, but eventually he moved to Leigh-on-Sea, which was a lot nearer to where I lived. While we were both at college we worked at Boston Hall Hotel on the seafront at Chalkwell on most weekends, serving at weddings, and also worked there over Christmas. As there were no buses or trains running over Christmas, I used to ride my bike all the way from Benfleet.

I passed all my exams at college, gaining a City and Guilds in Hotel and Catering as well as Silver Service waiting on tables. When I left college in 1957 I started working with Shell International Petroleum Company, which was in the City part of London. This was a very happy time of my life. The kitchen catered for 2,000 people and I was able to work in every section. It was very hard work but I loved it, and on Friday I would say, "Roll on Monday," so I could get back to work. Most of the chefs were men, and as most of them had come from working in the army and navy swearing was commonplace, but this did not bother me and I never picked up the habit. The kitchen ladies were lovely. Most of them were cockneys, but there was one Irish lady called Aggie, who was really funny and used to serve the fish. She was always shouting at the two chefs cooking the fish and chips. These two men were so different. The chip man, Mr Din, was from Africa and always wore a spotlessly clean white chef's uniform, which showed up well against his black skin. In contrast, Tom the fish man was a cockney, with a very untidy set of chef's clothes, his chef's hat pulled down over his face and his glasses hanging over his nose. It was there that I learnt how to carve a joint of meat and I would have to get 18 portions out of a leg of lamb. It is because of this training that I can still carve a leg of lamb even though I am totally blind. For cutting other meats we used an electric slicing machine. Fortunately, I was able to buy a smaller version for me to use at home, which I can use quite safely to this day.

When I was on omelette duty I would often make 300 omelettes in the space of two hours, on a large open range. We would break a case of eggs into a saucepan that was so large it had to be lifted by two people, and this would be mixed by machine before being positioned on a box alongside the cooking range. I would then get five omelette pans, line them up in a row and from a bowl of hot fat ladle a little into each pan. After getting the fat piping hot I would tip it out into the fat bowl and add a cupful of egg mixture to each pan, stirring each with a fork until the omelette was cooked.

I worked at Shell for five years, half the time in the kitchens located underneath Houndsditch Warehouses, and the rest of the time at St Swithins House, which was situated behind Mansion House in the middle of the City of London. I used to leave for work at six o'clock every morning, cycle to Benfleet Station and travel on the 6.25 a.m. early workmen's train. I would travel in the 'ladies only' carriage with friends I met on the train. I used to travel home on the 4.55 p.m. train with my dad to the first stop, Benfleet, and then cycle back home from there. My mum would have my tea ready for me, and then three nights a week I would get the bus to Westcliff and go to dancing at the Studio Ballroom. The Studio was run by a French couple called Madam and Professor, who were very good teachers but a bit old-fashioned in their ways. On one or two other nights I would go to the GLB. As my job was only five days a week I usually spent Saturday morning in bed catching up on sleep. On Sundays I would take a bus to Westcliff to attend church. I led a very active life.

One of the most memorable times in my life, and the one that gave me the greatest honour, was in 1957 when, as a member of the 2nd Westcliff GLB Company, I was in the team of four girls that won the first prize in the national home nursing competition. I was picked to receive the shield, which was awarded at the Royal Albert Hall in London. We had to walk down the long flight of stairs with the spotlight shining on us. We then had to walk across the floor up to the stage where Her Royal Highness the Duchess of Gloucester presented me with the shield. I took part in many GLB displays at the Royal Albert Hall, involving skipping, dancing, PE and marching. As I was the shortest girl I was usually at the front.

In 1958 I was asked by Major Baker, the commissioner of the GLB, if I would run a company at Hadleigh Baptist Church. This I did for six years until I went totally blind. My friend Peggy came to help me and we had a good time training the girls in all kinds of activities.

A telephone call I had in 1958 could have changed my life dramatically if I had taken up the offer that was made to me. Mrs Bennett, at whose guesthouse I had worked in Guernsey in 1954 and 1955, phoned me to say that she and her husband were suffering from cancer and wondered whether I would like to run the guesthouse for them. They gave me three days to decide, but because I was an only child and taking into account my sight problems I decided against it. I found out years later that both of them had died within six months and that Mrs Bennett's sister had tried to find me with a view to my taking up the offer to run the guesthouse, but she did not have my address. I often wondered if I had made the right decision.

I had finished going out with Peter Sawkins in April 1958 and did not want another serious boyfriend. I just wanted to have a good time. On my eighteenth birthday I caught up with a friend called Carol Fenton, who was sister to Ben, one of the boys I knew at college. She was training to be a nurse at Southend Hospital where I had been born. At the time her boyfriend was Mick Allen, who became my first husband five years later. When Carol went on holiday that July she asked me to look after Mick so that he would not go out with anyone else. I ended up looking after him for 25 years! At only 16 at that time, Mick was two years younger than me and I did not want to go out with him seriously for a while. Carol and I remained friends for many years, but she moved away when she got married.

1961 was a very memorable year for two reasons: I was 21 in March of that year and got engaged to Mick in the following December.

My birthday started with my mum waking me at 5.30 a.m. to give me my presents and cards. On the train to work the ladies I travelled with presented me with a cut-glass vase and a bouquet of flowers. One lady had bought me a lamp in the shape of giant cat with a large lampshade, which I still have. When I got to work the engineers gave me a great big key they had made and a trestle table had been erected in the ladies' room to put my presents on. My friend Linda, who was a cook with me, had bought me a needlework box filled with cottons and all sorts of sewing paraphernalia. Linda came home with me for the weekend, as my birthday was on the Friday but I was having my party on the Saturday. How we carried all those presents home I will never know.

When my grandfather died seven years earlier he had left me some money - only £100, but that was a lot of money to me. I decided to spend £75 on the party and hired the London Hotel in Southend High Street. I invited 75 friends and family, including Mick's family, and I made my own two-tier cake, icing it in yellow and lavender and topping it off with a real china vase. I had bought a gold lamé dress in Oxford Street in London for £10, which was a week's wages in those days. I still have the dress, but sadly it does not fit me anymore. My Auntie Maud, who had brought up my mum, bought me a gold bracelet, so with the rest of my granddad's money I bought three gold charms to adorn it. My party was just like a wedding and I was so pleased that I had spent all that money on making it such a special day, although at the time my father was not very happy about it.

During 1961 I transferred from Houndsditch to St Swithins House, which had a nicer kitchen, and again I worked in all sections, gaining a lot of experience. I was still working with my friend Linda, with whom I have kept in touch; in fact, her youngest child, Jolyon, is my godson. Linda was very good at pastry work and icing cakes. On her 21st birthday her mother took us to Covent Garden to see my first and only opera, called The Tales of Hoffman. Afterwards we went for tea in the Lyons Corner House, and it was one of those days I would never forget.

It was while I was working at Shell that our first cat, Blackie, died. He was 19 and a real family pet. The manageress in the Shell kitchen, Joan Long, who lived at Billericay, knew someone who had a litter of kittens to rehome, so she bought one for me. Although my mum and dad said they did not want another cat, when I walked in with this six-week-old kitten peeping out of my bag at them they could not resist him. We called him Shelly and he lived for 12 years, giving us all a lot of pleasure.

The other pet I had as a child was Sally. She was a golden spaniel, but she died with hard pad disease when she was only four years old. I was eight at the time and I can remember my mum telling me on the way home from school that Sally had been put to sleep. It just broke my heart and I never got over it. This was the main reason why I did not have a guide dog for seven years after I went blind. I just could not face the thought of coping with the death of another guide dog.

It was just after Christmas that I decided to leave Shell, as they were moving to a new building on the Embankment and the journey would have been too long to be feasible. I found alternative work near Piccadilly Circus, but after only three weeks I caught the flu and then a virus, falling very ill with pyelitis and cystitis, and I naturally lost my job. I thought I would give up catering and try to get my teaching diploma for dancing, so I spent all my savings on dancing lessons. Eventually I got another catering job more locally in Basildon. I was manageress in the canteen of Barton's Bakery, but on my doctor's advice I gave up this job after three months - it was like slave labour.

It was my dad who then saw a job advertised in the Daily Telegraph that looked too good to be true. Gallaher's, the tobacco company, were offering £10 a week for a directors' cook, involving very short hours and catering for between two and twenty directors each day. I applied for the job, but as I did not hear from them after more than two weeks of waiting I wrote again, which resulted in a telephone call from the manager, Mr Dovey. He told me that there had been a hundred applicants and that I was on the shortlist for an interview. However, as I seemed so keen, he invited me to go up there straight away, which I did and I got the job. I took over from a German lady who was extremely tidy and clean, but worked with her for four weeks before going it alone and she taught me so much. I had a lovely kitchen on the second floor and had a butler called John to help. There were also two waitresses called Daisy and Sylvia, who both knew my sight was bad and used to check the vegetables for me. All my ordering was done over the telephone, so it was quite easy for me to cope with.

Mick and I celebrated our engagement that December at a dance, run by my Uncle Bernard for the Canvey Yacht Club, at the Memorial Hall on Canvey Island. We had not set a wedding date, as we were both on low wages and did not have the money. Mick was then working as an electrician with Estuary Lighting and was living with his mother and sister at Eastwood, his father having died when he was three. He always rode his bike to save his bus fares. In the five years that I was going out with Mick, it was very hard to save for our home, as Mick was on a low wage and houses were not cheap, the average price for a three-bedroom house being around £3,000.

You will see that the first 24 years of my life were very active and most of the time quite happy. Although I did miss out by not having brothers and sisters, I was very lucky to have many nice friends, both male and female. Most of them knew nothing about my sight problem, however, so when I went totally blind on my wedding day it was a complete shock to everyone.

Although most of my teenage holidays were at the GLB camps, I did go with Peter Sawkins to Teignmouth in Devon and stayed at the Portland Hotel. In 1960, Carol and I went to Seefeld in Austrian Tyrol by boat and coach. This was to be my only journey abroad while I had my sight and so I was able to see the mountains and the beautiful scenery of Austria, which I will never forget. When I was 21 my dad hired a car and took me, my mum and a friend from work called Marian Peachey, who lived in nearby Rayleigh, on holiday to Scotland for two weeks, which again gave me the chance to see the Scottish scenery. We spent a weekend in Edinburgh and then travelled to Oban, where we stayed for ten days before making our way back home via the Lake District.

One of my friends from the dance studio was called Jeanette. Her boyfriend, Peter, who later became her husband, lived in Silversea Drive, Westcliff, and said there was a property for sale two doors away. So, after GLB one night in 1963, Mick, Peggy and I went to look at this house. It was in the middle of a block of three terraced houses and had been empty for 18 months. As soon as I opened the door I liked it and thought it would be just right for us, but I wasn't too taken with the back garden, as it was very small and had a large wall at the bottom that backed onto a builders' yard. As it turned out, however, it was an ideal garden for me to cope with when I went blind. We found out that the price was £2,750 and we contacted the estate agents to make an offer. After twelve weeks we contacted them again, as we had not heard anything, and asked why the owners had kept us waiting so long. It was at the time of the Profumo Affair, and we were told that the owner did not want to sell her house to a couple that were not married. She did not realise that we were young and would be getting married the following June. Once our situation was clarified we were able to go ahead. We made a deposit on the house and arranged a 20-year mortgage with payments commencing on 5 October. The following months were spent preparing for the wedding and getting the house ready for occupation. Mick would go to our new home after work to decorate the lounge, kitchen and bedroom before we moved in.

The plans for the wedding included booking Crowstone Church for the service and Westcliff Hotel for the reception. As our finances were very limited, we decided to go for a week's holiday to the Langham Hotel at Eastbourne and I bought some white lurex lace fabric for my wedding dress at Brightwell's in Southend High Street. My dress and the bridesmaids' dresses were made by a friend of my mother's. Two of my bridesmaids were to be Mick's sister Veronica and a friend called Susan Cowan, the daughter of an old friend of my mother's from the war years. My other little bridesmaid was Susan, the granddaughter of my mum's friend Mrs Ellwood, and she was only five. Not long before the wedding Mick's sister fell pregnant, which meant she could not be my bridesmaid, so at the last minute my friend Barbara Collison, who lived in my road, took her place. Barbara used to go dancing at the studio with me, and her boyfriend, Nick, and my boyfriend would see us girls on the bus to Benfleet and then stop and chat at the Elms, often eating fish and chips.

I had two other disappointments before the wedding. My godchild, Philip Bournes, who was six and was due to be a pageboy, was rushed into hospital to have his adenoids and tonsils out. Also, my friend Linda, who became an air hostess after leaving Shell, phoned to say that she could not come to the wedding because she had been put on the maiden flight of the Trident Aircraft.

I made my own wedding cake, but decided to have it iced by Gilbert's, my local baker. The heart-shaped tins had been specially made for me by the husband of Sylvia, who worked with me at Gallaher's. Although I had bought my headdress, I still had to sew on the veil myself, a task that I left to the wedding eve. This was the first time that I noticed that the vision in my good eye was failing; in fact it was so bleary that I had a job seeing what I was sewing. My dad telephoned my doctor and told him about my eye, but he thought it was probably nerves and would be better in the morning.

We had just enough money to buy a new bed, a cherry red dining suite and a hall carpet that was a lovely red colour. Mick's' mother had bought us a kitchen table and four chairs for our engagement and wedding present. My grandma gave us an old three-piece suite that belonged to her but was in very good condition, so we were very lucky. We brought my dressing table and wardrobe from my bedroom at home, which lasted us for many years until we could afford a proper bedroom suite.

We thought it would be easier if my dad took our suitcase to Victoria Station in London on the Friday to save us from having to carry it on the Saturday. Nearly all the clothes we possessed were in that case. We had invited 86 friends and family to the wedding and had booked a band to play at the reception – the same one that had performed at my 21st birthday party.

We had originally booked the wedding for 2 o'clock, but I thought it would be too long to wait for dinner, so at the last minute we moved the time forward an hour. This time change was to prove quite significant, as you will see ...

CHAPTER 3 – A WEDDING TO REMEMBER

The wedding day arrived. It was 6 June and the anniversary of D-Day, and it was to be the day that changed my life completely. After getting up and dressed I had my breakfast and read my wedding cards, as the bleariness of the night before had cleared as the doctor had said it would.

I walked to the bus stop and caught the bus to Chalkwell to have my hair set at the hairdresser's. Fortunately, I decided on the spur of the moment to have my hair cut short. The Carlton salon, where I had been going for many years, was located not far from our new house, and Mr William Poles, my hairdresser, was to act as my MC at the wedding reception, as he had done at my 21st birthday. Mr Ellwood collected me by car from the hairdresser's and took me back home to Benfleet to prepare for the wedding.

I arrived home to find the three bridesmaids already dressed in their blue satin long dresses. I had a quick sandwich and then went into my little bedroom to change into my wedding dress. I had only just finished when the photographer called me to go into the garden for some pre-wedding shots. As my dressing table had already been taken to the new house, I had no mirror in my bedroom and was unable to see myself as a bride. I had intended to use the mirror in my mum's bedroom but there was no time left, as once the photographer had finished it was time for me and my dad to make the 20-minute drive to the church. Jimmy and Pam Bournes were also in the garden to take a video of me. It was their son, Philip, who should have been my pageboy. Pam had lived next door to me before she got married and had been like a sister to me, and she was to be a wonderful friend to me over the next few years of my life, although her life was shortened not too many years later.

The sun was shining brightly as my dad and I walked down our long footpath to the car that would take us to the church. We arrived on time, and as I walked up the aisle on the arm of my dad I could see all my friends waiting eagerly to witness my marriage. Like any bride I was nervous but I felt fine and very happy. The service, which went well, was taken by the Revd Wallace Lawrence, whom I had known ever since I joined the church in 1956 and as a member of the GLB. After the service we went out into the minister's office to sign the register, and this would be the last thing I wrote with my sight. So from Jill Griffith I became Jill Allen.

The next few hours were like a nightmare and, in fact, I'd had dreams prior to the wedding of what was going to happen. Photographs were taken outside the church and then we stepped into the car that would take us to the reception. Before we left, Dave wanted to take our picture as we sat in the car. I can remember that picture so well, and it was the last one taken while I still had my sight. We then drove the short distance to the Westcliff Hotel for the reception. The car pulled up at the front of the hotel and we walked up the short flight of steps and into the hallway. As we proceeded down the corridor to the reception area, my good eye started to go bleary again and the strip lights in front of me were dazzling. We stopped at the end of the corridor to await the arrival of our 86 guests.

We greeted everyone individually and then Dave the photographer ushered us into the reception room to have our picture taken cutting the cake. It was at that point, as we walked towards the cake, that the vision in my eye went completely and the pain started. I told Mick not to tell anyone, as I did not want to spoil their day. Madam and Professor, our teachers from the dance studio, were nearby and started to fuss around, insisting that I take some smelling salts. These made me feel sick, and so after sitting down to eat I soon wanted to leave the table. My mum took me out to the toilet and I was sick, but I told my mum not to tell anyone and went back to the table. I sat through the whole meal and then made a speech thanking everyone for coming and for the lovely presents.

We started the dancing off, but I felt so ill that we went up to the room we had booked so that we had somewhere to change our outfits before leaving for our honeymoon. It was suggested that I should take a ride out in the car to get some fresh air, so Mr Ellwood drove Mick and I along the seafront to Chalkwell and back. I can remember hearing the noise of all the day trippers enjoying themselves on this very hot day. The car ride made no difference to my vision and the pain was getting worse. Eventually we left the reception early and made our way to Westcliff Station to catch the train to London. All I can remember is sitting on a train packed with day trippers, who were all looking at me because I was covered with confetti. I had changed into a bright pink suit, which had been made for me by the same lady that had made my wedding dress, and I had bought a hat to match my outfit. I cannot remember much about the journey, but when we got to Victoria Station Mick had to leave me while he went to collect our case, which my dad had taken to the 'left luggage' area the previous day. We had considered not travelling to London but, because all our clothes were in that case, we decided to go ahead. I kept thinking that my eye would get better as it had previously. Waiting for Mick was the most frightening experience of that day, and the journey to Eastbourne was not very pleasant as I was feeling sick and was in pain. I can remember travelling in the taxi from the station to the hotel, and all I could see were flashing lights in my eyes.

We arrived at the Langham Hotel quite late, so we went straight to bed. Mick and I were both very upset that the day had gone so sadly wrong, as we had saved up for five years to get married and had spent all that time preparing for the wedding and getting the house ready. I was so very ill and in so much pain that Mick eventually asked the hotel to get me a doctor. He arrived quite quickly and, after examining me, he sent for an ambulance. This scenario was the part of the dream I'd had a few weeks earlier, when I had heard the ambulance ringing its bell along Eastbourne seafront.

The ambulance men lifted me into a carrying stretcher and took me to St Mary's Hospital. After many tests, and suspicions of a possible tumour, it was decided that I had acute glaucoma. A nurse sat with me day and night, putting drops in my eye to try to reduce the high fluid pressure within my eye. When she first saw me she was very upset as I still had confetti in my hair from the wedding.

I can remember very well that on that Sunday morning someone came into the ward and played an organ. They played the hymn "There is a Green Hill Far Away", which had been one of my favourites at St Margaret's School and I had sung it many times at Sunday School at Benfleet Methodist Church.

Mick had telephoned my mum and dad and they travelled down that Sunday morning to see me. The doctor decided that I needed an operation and felt that I should go either to Moorfields Eye Hospital, where I had been a patient for all my life, or to Southend General Hospital, where I had been born 24 years earlier. I knew that there was an ophthalmic consultant at Southend called Mr Choyce so I chose to go there, as it would be expensive and difficult for Mick to travel to Moorfields each day.

On the Monday morning, when I was feeling a little better, I started the long journey back to Southend Hospital, where I had to spend the next three weeks - not the sort of honeymoon we had planned. I was transferred from Eastbourne by ambulance and train, and it was quite amusing that we caught the 4 o'clock train from Fenchurch Street station, which was the train I took back home from work. The carriage had been reserved for me and bore the label 'Mrs Allen', which sounded very odd. Once I arrived at Southend Hospital I was put in a small room with just two beds. In the other bed was a very young girl called Cynthia, who was 14 years old and was having implants in her eyes. I always called Cynthia my first guide dog, as she would always take me to the toilet and help me around the ward. She also helped to cheer me up.

It was quite strange that my ward was just down the corridor from where I had been born, although Southend Hospital was no longer used as a maternity hospital. During the first few years of the war one ward was used for that purpose.

As I had been admitted as an emergency, the doctors decided that Mr Choyce should be brought back from a conference to make an immediate assessment. When he arrived he took one look at me and said, "What a mess," and asked me why I gone ahead with the wedding with my eye in such a terrible state.

Even though I told him I had worked until the previous Friday as a cook in London and had read my wedding day cards, he would not listen. His attitude really upset me, as I did not know what was going to happen and could not understand why I should have postponed the wedding.

I can remember very well the first meal I was given in hospital. I was sitting in an armchair next to my bed when the nurse brought me the first dinner that I was well enough to eat and asked me if I would like my food cutting up. I felt quite shocked and said, "No thank you," as I did not want anyone else touching my food. This was my first experience of people thinking that because I was blind I could not do the ordinary things in life that sighted people take for granted.

My operation was scheduled for the following Friday, 19 June. I had a general anaesthetic, so all I can remember is waking up in my bed in that small room after the operation, unable to see anything as I had bandages on my eyes. When Mr Choyce came in to see me and removed the bandages to examine my eye I was thrilled to be able to see the flowers at the end of my bed. These were pink and white carnations that Mr Dovey, who had been my boss at Gallaher's, had sent from Guernsey. We had always had these flowers every week and Mr Dovey knew how much they meant to me.

Mr Choyce said that my future looked promising but that I would have to become a private patient for him to help me any further with my sight. Naturally, this was a shock to me, as we had no money and had a mortgage to pay, and I did not know if I would be able to go back to work again. I was very upset by Mr Choyce's suggestion and the fact that he said if I did not pay to be treated privately then I would be like a ship passing in the night. Another doctor, Dr Naffie, was very kind and tried to comfort me. I had other friends who were nurses at the hospital and they tried to ease my anxieties and encourage me to carry on.

After seeing those flowers I was full of hope and telephoned Mick and my mum to tell them I could see a little bit. Prayers were said for me at Benfleet Methodist Church and Crowstone Church. However, the next day when Mr Choyce removed the bandages my eye had returned to its pre-operation state and I simply could not understand it.

Mick and I talked about selling our new house to get the money to pay Mr Choyce for private treatment, but it all seemed too much to cope with. Mick had taken two weeks' holiday for our wedding and had spent most of that time at the hospital with me. His boss, Mr Haynes, was very understanding and let him have an extra week. Mr Haynes also bought me a small radio, which cheered me up no end, as I loved my music. Radio Caroline had just started broadcasting at that time and I knew all the chart hits and the presenters. 'My Guy' by Mary Wells was number 1, and Julie Rogers' 'The Wedding' was another top-10 hit. I recall those two in particular as both had quite appropriate themes at that time. As there were no earphones available, I was constantly being told off for having Radio Caroline on all the time.

I had never liked taking tablets but soon learnt to get used to them, as I had to take 16 at a time. During those three weeks in hospital I took over 1,500 tablets. After a few days I was transferred to a larger ward, but I have no recollection of the other patients there. I know I missed Cynthia and believed she had gone home. I have kept friends with her and she is still living on Canvey Island, but now she is totally blind like me.

While in that ward I had a visit from one of my grandfather's sisters, Cissy Patience, and her husband Reg. They had been my favourite auntie and uncle, and I was so thrilled that they had travelled all the way from Enfield to see me. They told me about the voluntary work they did in Enfield for blind people, including a talking newspaper that they would deliver to blind people's houses each week. I thought this was a good idea and eventually campaigned for a talking newspaper to be started in Southend. In 2002 the Enfield talking newspaper celebrated its 40th anniversary, so this must have been the first one of its kind in the country.

Another patient in the eye ward at that time was Vic Price, who lived near Uncle Bernard and Grandma on Canvey Island. He'd had an accident while demolishing the Chatman Lighthouse and eventually lost his sight completely. By coincidence, he was with me at Leamington Spa seven years later when we were both training with our first guide dogs. His dog's name was Gilda. However, there was a lot of readjusting to do before I got my first guide dog.

CHAPTER 4 – READJUSTING

When I was well enough to leave hospital it was decided that we should stay at my mum's for three weeks to recuperate prior to moving into our new house. Mick went back to work and travelled each day from Benfleet to his shop at Leigh-on-Sea, where he was an electrician. As the weather was nice and hot I spent most of the time sitting in our lovely garden listening to my radio, and that was when I first found an interest in tennis. It was Wimbledon fortnight and so I was able to follow the whole two weeks. I do not think I have ever had the time to do that since. I was learning to move around without my sight and also tried knitting again, discovering that I could actually knit better without sight than when I had a little sight.

During that first week I received a telephone call from my friend Marion's mum, who said she would be willing to give me one of her eyes if it would help me. Unfortunately, this was not possible as my optic nerve had been badly damaged by the measles and with the effects of the glaucoma as well there was nothing that could be done. Marion's mum was a lovely lady, who never went out as she had ulcerated legs, but she was always happy and whenever I visited she always made me feel welcome. I really appreciated her offer to try to help me see again.

I received no counselling at the hospital regarding my loss of sight and I was not visited by anyone from Social Services, so I had no rehabilitation and was not aware of any aids that might help me. As my mother had always tried to hide my visual disability, because of her own guilty conscience, she did not tell anyone I had gone blind. My friends would ask after me and she would just tell them I had got married, making no mention of the fact that I had gone blind. I was told years later that Bill Cox, a home teacher for the blind, had tried to visit me at Benfleet, but my mum had told him I did not live there anymore and they could not trace me because my surname and address had changed following my wedding. This was a case of my mother being over-protective, and this happens so often to people that have lost their sight.

After three weeks I went back to our house in Silversea Drive, where I had got to learn to live both as a wife and as a totally blind person. I was still getting over the trauma of the wedding drama and my subsequent operation, but now I had the worry of how we were going to pay the mortgage and the other bills if I could not return to work. We had based our mortgage on two incomes, as Mick was earning £12 a week and I was earning £10 a week. Fortunately, Gallaher's paid me for a whole year, which really saved us from having to sell the house. We even considered converting the house into two flats, as it was large enough, as a last resort if we were unable to pay the bills. Also on our minds was the possibility of paying Mr Choyce for private treatment if that would get my sight back. I did attend the eye clinic regularly, but it was quite clear that they could not do anything for my sight. For the first few years I was able to distinguish light and dark, but could not see colours or anything else. Later, however, I developed shingles in my eye, which took away my light perception.

My dad was still working in London and used to telephone me every day from work. He contacted our building society and arranged for our mortgage to be paid over 40 years instead of 20, which reduced our monthly outlay. I never went out on my own and had very few visitors. Mick's working hours were 8 till 5, but he would come home for lunch every day. We could not afford a television, but Mrs Smith (Peter's mother), who lived just two doors away, used to invite us round once or twice a week to watch theirs.

Our financial instability was very worrying, and I was upset that I could not go out to work to help pay the bills. Our money worries actually caused me more distress than the fact that I had gone blind. I just used to love my work, as well as my dancing and running the GLB company, but being able to do any of these activities again seemed like an impossible dream.

When I returned to our new home in Westcliff, I found it totally different having no sight as opposed to the poor sight that I'd had for the first 24 years of my life.

The first few weeks at home I spent listening to my radio and knitting. While I was at my mum's she was able to read the pattern and measure the knitting for me, but now I was on my own I found it frustrating. If only I had known about a Braille tape measure, which I found out about four years later. Although I had been a regular member of my church, I was very surprised and sorry that I was not visited at home by either the minister or anyone else for months.

I had to learn to walk around the house safely. I still have to remember that there is one step beyond where the banister ends, although I have a handrail on the other side of the stairs, which makes it a lot easier. This was installed when I slipped down the last few stairs one day while carrying the cat. I only cracked my ribs and, although it was very painful for a few weeks, I did not have to go to hospital. It certainly taught me never to rush up and down the stairs like I used to.

One of the biggest hazards in the house for a blind person is the doors. Visitors would often leave them half open and, of course, I walked into them. It is better to keep them completely closed or wide open. My poor dad would often leave my kitchen door open, and I would walk straight down the hall and hit my head on it. We eventually took the door off and replaced it with a sliding door, but one day the cat got stuck under it and we ended up removing that door completely.

The cat, Buttons, certainly had nine lives and lived until he was 19. Although he was Jacqueline's cat he was very affectionate with me. He witnessed many of my tears over the years. He was Jacqueline's second cat, her first one being Sparky, a ginger cat that Mick and I had got her for her fifth birthday. She had always wanted a cat, and although we could not afford much we went to the People's Dispensary for Sick Animals (PDSA) to find one that needed rehoming. Sparky was only six weeks old and we put him in a little basket and gave it to her in bed on her birthday morning.

One of the things I missed, and still do, was being able to look out of the window to identify the source of any noise I heard, and I will only open my front door if I am certain of the caller. In 1974 I arranged to have a password system with the Gas and

Electricity Boards, so that I knew who was at the door. This is now common practice all over the country.

I also still miss looking in the mirror, for instance when brushing or combing my hair. Sometimes when I have been to a salon the hairdresser has held up a mirror for me to look at the back of my hair, like they do for their other customers, forgetting that I cannot see. Edna, my current hairdresser, does not have this problem as she comes to my home and does my hair in the kitchen, where we have no mirror. Although I used to like to walk round to the local salon, this arrangement fits in well with my busy diary.

Something I still miss is being able to pick up the post each day and read it. I know we have a lot of material on tape and CD, but there are simple things like the local free paper and adverts that I cannot read.

Friends and family have been very thoughtful over the years in their attempts to buy me the types of birthday and Christmas cards that enable me to feel the picture, although it is still frustrating that I cannot see and read all the cards. Although my husband Alvin can see to read large print he cannot read handwriting. This is where all my friends come in to help. There is always a pile of papers to read in our house.

The Brownies at my Church, Chalkwell Methodist, each Christmas since 2004 have made me about 40 tactile cards for me to send to my friends who are blind. This is such a kind and practical way that children can help blind people.

CHAPTER 5 – LIFE AS A NEW MOTHER

It was not long after the start of my new life as a blind person that I discovered I was expecting a baby. This gave me something to live for and took the place of the busy, active life that I had lost since going blind.

The first doctor that knew I was pregnant was Mr Choyce, the eye consultant. He said straight away that I should have an abortion, as the drugs I was taking for my eye might affect the baby. He advised me to see a gynaecologist, which I did soon after. The specialist Mr Sutton was very nice to me and assured me that everything should be all right if I wanted to go ahead and have the baby. I was worried, however, because a lot of thalidomide babies were being born at that time and I wondered if my baby would be similarly affected.

My mum was very upset to hear about my pregnancy and really did not want me to have the baby, but I was determined to go ahead having received Mr Sutton's reassurance. I spent a lot of time in Rochford Maternity Hospital, as I gained a lot of weight and the doctors wanted to monitor the pressure in my eye. This hospital was much further for Mick to travel to visit me. We could not afford a car so he rode his bicycle everywhere, and he used to ring the bell on it to let me know he was arriving.

Most of my time in the hospital was spent knitting. I used to knit model poodles, and all the nursing sisters wanted one for their cars. I used to stuff them with kapok, which made such a mess that I had to tidy up before the doctors did their rounds. I met some lovely people there who helped me walk around the ward and took me to the toilet. One of the sisters was Jean Hall, who was in the GLB, and she had visited me in Southend Hospital when I went blind. She came to see me every day while I was in Rochford, even on her days off. She eventually became my daughter's godmother, and no one could have fulfilled that role better than Jean. Apart from Mum, Dad, Mick and Jean, another regular visitor was Mrs Sawkins (my former boyfriend's mother).

As the time approached for the birth of our baby, I did wonder how I was going to cope and what I would do if I had another child. So, about a week before the birth, I raised the issue of family planning with Mr Sutton, the gynaecologist. I was hoping that I would be able take the new form of contraception, the pill, which most of the other women on the ward were going to use. Unfortunately, I was told that the pill would not be suitable because of my eye condition, and Mr Choyce was brought in to see me. Speaking from the end of my bed, he said if I were to have any more children my eye would not improve. So, three days before the birth, it was decided that it would be better for me to be sterilised. After discussing this with Mick, we agreed that this should be done while I was having the planned Caesarean. I have regretted this decision ever since, and I think the hospital were wrong to recommend this procedure and should have spent more time discussing it with us, and not just before the birth of our child. Further annoyance in this respect was caused after a visit to Moorfields Eye Hospital a couple of years later, when the eye consultants asked why had I been sterilised. There was nothing they could do for my sight, because my optic nerve had been destroyed by the measles. It was simply that the doctors at Rochford Hospital did not think that a blind person could or should bring up a child. This was quite obvious when their first reaction was to recommend an abortion. I would hope that the attitude of doctors has now changed. If my blindness had been hereditary then that would have been a different matter.

I felt quite well when I was taken down to the operating theatre to have our baby. Mick was able to come with me but was not allowed into the theatre until after the operation. When I came round from the operation I was told that I had a baby daughter and that she was fine. I was transferred to a private room and I could hear the baby crying, and even though I was in a lot of pain they gave me the baby to hold. She spent her first few hours in the premature baby unit, which was standard procedure for babies born by Caesarean section. She had a healthy weight of eight pounds and was soon at the side of my bed in a cot.

It was not long before Mick sent me a basket of flowers - mostly freesias and the scent was wonderful. For many years he would refill the same basket with the same kind of flowers on Jacqueline's birthday. We chose Mary as her second name and she was born with red hair. When my mum first saw her she said that Jacqueline had the same colour hair as Adrian, the boy who lived next door to me at Benfleet, which enabled me to visualise what she looked like.

Unfortunately, I could not breastfeed her for very long as it was affecting the pressure in my eye and causing a lot of pain. I was shown how to wash, change and feed Jacqueline and then allowed to do it all on my own. I stayed in hospital for ten days and then it was time for me to go home. While I was in hospital my dad had bought his very first car. It was only cheap as he could not afford much, but he knew it would help me get about with the baby. So one of his first trips in 'Smokey', as he called the car, was to collect Jacqueline and me from hospital.

I was discharged from hospital without any arrangements for help at home, and it was not until my GP, Dr Pearson, came to visit me six weeks later, after my postnatal, that a home help was organised for five days a week from nine until one. My first home help was Sylvia, but she only lasted for a few weeks. She was a Jehovah's witness and kept telling me that if I followed her religion I would get my sight back, which caused me a great deal of distress. Then I had Cissie for a few months. She was a lovely lady from Newcastle and we used to have a good laugh. I had never heard of a home help and did not know what they were going to do. I could do all my own cooking, ironing and looking after Jacqueline, so the home help would do the washing. We did not have a washing machine in the first few years, so everything had to be washed by hand and put through a wringer. The home help also did the cleaning and some shopping, although Mick and I would go on a Friday evening to the local shops and get most of the shopping for the week.

Jacqueline was about 14 months old when my third home help arrived. She was called Pat and she remained as my home help until Jacqueline was 12 years old, when I was forced to choose between paying for a home help or sending Jacqueline on school trips. I always tried to put her needs first and I thought it was important that she went on school visits. The doctor also arranged for someone from Social Services to talk to me about my blindness and see how they could help. They asked me if I would like to learn Braille and if I wanted a white stick or a talking book. I said that all I wanted at that time was something that would measure the milk I had put in Jacqueline's bottle. I received such a device four years later when I no longer needed it. I said I would try a talking book, but that did not arrive for 18 months, by which time I was doing other things. I told them that I did not want a white stick as I did not intend going out on my own, and that I did not want to learn Braille as I was hoping to get my sight back one day. I was not told that there were knitting books available in Braille, which might have given me an incentive to learn it at that time.

I was aware that people did not think I would be able to cope with a baby, so I tried to prove them wrong by letting Jacqueline do all the normal things that other children of her age were doing. I knew I had to prevent her from having accidents in the home, but at the same time I did not want to be too over-protective. My training in the GLB had stood me in good stead and I was able to put into practice all the things I had learnt about safety in the home, first aid and hygiene. We had two child gates - one at the bottom of the stairs and one at the entrance to the kitchen - to stop Jacqueline from climbing up the stairs or entering the kitchen while I was dishing up the dinner. However, she still had to learn about danger and would be in the kitchen with me, and at 18 months old she would sit on a chair at the end of the sink and pass me the dishes to wipe. We had an indoor swing and a rocking horse that she would move from room to room, usually accompanied by singing 'Grocer Jack', so she got plenty of exercise. My dad would often take her to the park, where she would play on the swings and slides.

Right from when Jacqueline was born I always bathed her myself, and I always dressed her in a fresh set of clothes each day. This was to ensure that she was always clean. When she was a little baby we had a small bath that slotted into a frame. Mick cut some legs off a chair so that I could sit down at her level.

I would get all her clean clothes ready before I prepared the water, always putting some cold water in the bath first. I even do that today, as you can never be certain how hot the water from the hot tap will be. When Jacqueline was older and used the large bath, I would still work in the same way, and would leave her in the cot until the water was ready. When she was wearing nappies, which in those days were made of terry towelling that had to be washed and reused, it was very time consuming. It took hours without a washing machine, and we would dry them in front of our open coal fire as we had no central heating for the first year.

Peter's father had bought me an apron when I was 16, and I had never imagined how useful it would become once I had gone blind. It had really large pockets, so I was able to collect and move things from room to room, as necessary, as I walked around the house. It was particularly useful for nappy changing, as I used to store the large nappy pin in the pocket while I was actually changing the nappy, which kept it safely out of the way. I would always close the pin when I took it off, and when pinning up the clean nappy I would put my hand between Jacqueline's skin and the nappy so that the pin would not dig into her. The only time she really had an accident was when a health visitor came to check on her. She took her nappy off and left her lying on my bed with the nappy pin left open. I was very cross and said that all the staff should have been trained properly, but they obviously were not.

I had caught the measles that had caused so much damage to my eye at a baby clinic, so my mother did not like me taking Jacqueline to a clinic. I only went when Jacqueline needed vaccinations, and my own doctor would come to see me if there were any other problems.

It was when Jacqueline was about 18 months old that there was a knock at the door - it was my friend Peggy. I had not seen her since her wedding in 1963 as she had gone to live in Africa, so she did not know I had gone blind or had a baby. She was very shocked and upset and never got over it, so I have not been able to keep in touch with her. Peggy's parents had moved from Benfleet to Devon and suggested that we went there for a holiday, as they knew we could not afford one. Peggy had brought a parrot back from Africa and wanted it taking down to Devon, so we went. It was such a difficult journey. I still was not using a white stick, so no one knew I was blind, and on top of that Jacqueline was still in her pushchair and we had the parrot in a cage. How Mick coped I will never know, but the return journey was easier without the parrot.

It was around this time that I met Colin Wells. He lived near where Mick worked and was a totally blind man. As I had not met a sightless person at that time I was quite nervous when he came to see me, and I was amazed he had found his way to my house. He said he would take me for a walk around the block and, without time to think about it, off we went. As we walked Colin commented on the things we were passing, such as trees, cars and lamp posts, and I was convinced he could see, but when we got back I found out that he really was totally blind.

As I did not have a large family, my friends meant a lot to me and still do. My friend Jeanette used to come every Tuesday and have lunch with me, and she would sometimes take me out for a walk. Even if the weather was bad she would never let me down, and she came every week until her own children were born.

One of my very best friends was Pam, who lived next door to me in Southview Road where I lived from 1951 until I got married in 1964. Pam was ten years my senior and was just like a sister to me. She'd had a nervous breakdown when she was quite young, before she got married to Jimmy who was a plumber. She was a hairdresser and would often do my hair for me. I went to her wedding, and when she had her first child, who was a lovely boy named Philip, I was so surprised and thrilled when she asked me to be his godmother. I was only 18 at the time and the christening was held at St Mary's Church in Benfleet. I can remember having to hold Philip in the service, and this was such a proud moment in my life. Pam and Jimmy went on to have another son called Graham three years later, followed another three years later by a daughter called Alison. It was only a couple of years after that Pam found out she had cancer. I had always joked with Pam about smoking, as I hated it and I had never had even one cigarette and yet I had cooked for the directors of

Gallaher's the cigarette company for two years until I went blind. Pam was the only person who continued to treat me exactly the same after I went blind, and she encouraged me to carry on with all my interests, such as dancing and the GLB. I could always confide in her about any of my personal problems, so when I discovered she did not have long to live I was devastated. When she died Philip was eleven, Graham seven and Alison only three. My own daughter was five at the time and I just could not imagine what Jacqueline would do without me. An old friend, Enid, from school took me to the funeral and I was so upset. I have never got over Pam's death and often think about her and what a wonderful person she was. She would be so proud of her eldest son Philip, whom I sometimes meet on the train when returning from London. Her husband Jimmy died only a few years ago, and when I went to the funeral each one of the children just put their hand on me as they walked up behind the coffin. I just thought that was a kind gesture and what nice adults they had become.

Pam's death upset me more than going blind. When I went blind my reaction was, "Why should God do this to me?" I felt the same when Pam died, but in my case I can see that my experience has helped other people in some ways, whereas I could see no reason why Pam should be taken away so tragically from her devoted husband and three young children. I did not go to church for weeks following her funeral.

Mick and I used to push Jacqueline in the pram all the way to Crowstone Church, which was a good 20-minute walk away, and when Jacqueline was old enough she went to the Sunday School. She was about three years old, and it was there I met a new friend.

Jill Welsh was the Sunday School teacher and she offered to take me to the dancing school attended by her daughter, who was a year older than Jacqueline. From that time on we have been good friends, and Jill has helped me in so many ways.

Jacqueline was three-and-a-half years old when I decided to take her for a walk on my own around our block. She knew she had to hold my hand and be good. It was when we arrived back at our gate that a lady from down the road, who had been watching me, came and spoke to me. Her name was Maureen and she had a little girl the same age as Jacqueline. We became good friends for many years until she moved to another part of town. Her daughter, Julie, became good friends with Jacqueline and they played together and went to the same school for many years.

It was when Jacqueline was three that Brian and Sheila became our new next-door neighbours. They had a daughter named Christine, who was a year younger than Jacqueline. She would come round and play with Jacqueline and also went camping with us when the children were older. Christine had a hearing problem, and so we would relate very well to each other with our different disabilities. Christine was one of five children but was the only one with a hearing defect.

I had stopped everything when I went blind, really because I did not think that a blind person could do the activities and work that I had enjoyed as a sighted person. Therefore, I was surprised when Joyce, a captain of the GLB at Hadleigh Congregational Church, told me she was leaving and asked if I would take over the company as soon as possible. So, with my mother's help, I became captain and was once again very proud to be wearing my uniform. One of the girls there changed my life in more ways that she would realise. Her name was Graham and she suggested that we collect silver paper in order to get me a guide dog. At that time Blue Peter was collecting for guide dogs, but as we did not have a television I did not know this. The subject of my having a guide dog had never been raised before. Graham and her sister Lisa were lovely girls, and I gave them as much help as I could as their parents were splitting up. One Friday evening their father phoned me and asked about the forthcoming church parade, as I would be taking part and carrying the flag. He thought that this was quite an achievement, as I would be marching through the streets. I explained that it would be quite easy, as I would have sighted officers next to me to guide me. I wondered why he was so interested, and then I found out that he was a reporter for the local newspaper. He asked me how long I had been blind and how it had come about, and when I explained my story he nearly had a fit and was

38

astounded that they did not know about it at the newspaper. It was just something you did not talk about in those days.

A reporter named Val Flatley came to see me and wrote a long article for the paper, which included pictures of me hanging my washing on the line and carrying the flag for the Girls' Brigade parade. From then on the Southend Standard and the Southend Pictorial kept a close eye on my activities and they have helped me with many of my campaigns. I did not know for many years that it was Val Flatley who had sent that first article to the In Touch programme on Radio 4, which led to my making regular broadcasts on the show.

I carried on knitting and really enjoyed it, making Mick all his jumpers and many of Jacqueline's woolly clothes. But, apart from sewing up my knitted garments and sewing on the odd button, I had not done any dressmaking since going blind. That was all to change, however, when one year I decided to enter Jacqueline in Southend Carnival's fancy dress competition. At the time Sir Alec Rose was circumnavigating the world on a sailing boat called Lively Lady, so I thought I would use this as the theme for Jacqueline's outfit. I did not know how I was going to achieve this, but decided to make her a simple dress in dark green taffeta and decorate it with roses made from crêpe paper. Peggy, the mother of one of the boys at Jacqueline's dancing classes, offered to cut out the dress pattern for me, which was very helpful, and then I did the machining myself. I was quite surprised that I could machine straighter than when I had some vision in one eye.

I can remember making my first rose on a Saturday afternoon, when Mick had gone to do some work for a friend. I had a packet of pink crêpe paper, a small tea plate, a pair of scissors and a needle and cotton. Within a short time I had made my first rose, which was to be the first of many thousands that I would make over the next ten years. I ended up with 100 roses for the dress and a large one to adorn the hat I had made. Mick decorated Jacqueline's little three-wheeled tricycle with the flags of the world and made a boat-shaped frame to go around the bike. We bought a globe and fixed it onto the boat, together with another 100 roses. On the morning of the fancy dress competition

Jacqueline rode her decorated bike the short distance to Chalkwell Park, located at the top of our road. What a surprise we all had when she came first in the competition and was presented with her prize by the Mayor of Southend!

In the afternoon we went round to Leigh Road to watch the carnival procession. Unfortunately it rained, so we had to cover the whole boat with Jacqueline inside it, but everyone could see her and people said she looked really sweet.

This experience gave us the bug for doing more for the carnival, and so each Christmas I would think up a topical idea for that year's float.

By coincidence, it was about the same time that Val sent her article to the BBC that I found the In Touch show on the radio. The first programme I heard was about a new form of mobility training, involving teaching a blind person to walk with a long white cane, that had come over to the UK from America. I thought this might help me to get around, as I was wondering at the time how I was going to take Jacqueline to school. This was to be my first campaign. I wrote to the BBC to find out all about it and how I could receive some training. I was informed that it was a six-month course and would be held in Birmingham, which was out of the question for me because of Jacqueline. I therefore wrote to my Council to suggest that they send someone on the training course, so that they could qualify as a mobility officer and then train not only me but also the 600 other blind people living in the Southend area. The area only had three home teachers for the blind at that time and they did not teach mobility.

So, one year later, Mr Denny was employed by Southend Council as the first mobility officer in the county of Essex. I was the first person he trained, together with Alan Piper, who went to my church and was a brilliant pianist. Alan played the piano at most of my birthday parties and at my wedding to Alvin, and he also played the organ at my dad's funeral. Mr Denny had not quite finished mobility training with me when Jacqueline started nursery school, and although it was only a short walk to the local church, with only one side of the road to cross, I was still nervous and my social worker promised that she would meet me there and walk back with me. We had already walked the route a couple of times. Jacqueline was four when she started nursery school, and on that first morning the journey there went fine. However, I waited for the social worker to meet me as arranged and she did not turn up, so I had to make my way back on my own. This was the first walk I had done unaccompanied and I was very cross at being let down.

A lot of the children that Jacqueline met at nursery school moved on to the same primary school the following September.

CHAPTER 6 – ENTERING THE MEDIA SPOTLIGHT

Following my letter to the In Touch programme and their receipt of a copy of the article from the Southend Standard, they telephoned me and asked if I would go on the show to talk about being a Girls' Brigade officer despite my blindness. It was 1968, and this was the first broadcast of hundreds to come. The programme's producer, Thena Heshel, came to my home to interview me for the show and, on finding out that I had been a cook prior to losing my sight, she asked me if I would like to contribute some cookery items for the show, which I did for many years. She brought with her a lot of pieces of equipment designed to help blind people, all available from the RNIB. I was not aware of any of these aids at that time. One was a measuring jug with raised lines, and this would have been so helpful when I first went blind.

At this time Thena also wrote the first In Touch Handbook. In the book she described how I had brought up Jacqueline even though I had been offered an abortion and was sterilised after her birth. I received many calls from health visitors and other blind people after the book was published, telling me that they had experienced the same attitude from doctors and family members towards blind people and their capacity to have children, some them having agreed to have abortions.

Just before my first In Touch programme, I did a live telephone interview with Jimmy Young, one of many that I did over the years for his radio show. Initially, I talked about going blind on my wedding day and the everyday practicalities, but future programmes dealt with my campaign issues.

David Scott Blackhall was the presenter of the In Touch programme at that time, and we had both been sent a gadget to help with pouring a cup of tea. It was called a liquid level indicator and had been designed by Mr Burndrett. His father was blind and he could see that he needed something to help with this task.

David and I discussed this invention on the programme, and as a representative of the National Federation of the Blind (NFB) on the RNIB council I approached the RNIB with a view to selling it. However, I was told by an officer that there would be insufficient demand for such an item and it would not be worth the RNIB stocking it. In actuality, every time we mentioned this gadget on the programme Mr Burndrett received many sales enquiries.

In addition to the In Touch programme, at that time the BBC started to set up special programmes for blind people on local radio stations. In those days we did not have local radio in Essex but Kent did, so about once a month I would travel to Gravesend to do a slot with Radio Kent. It was quite a journey. I had my normal half-hour walk to Chalkwell station, took a train to Tilbury riverside station and finally caught the ferry across the Thames. To save me the journey to the studio in Maidstone, the harbour master used to let the presenter interview me in his hut.

Eventually a commercial radio station was set up in Southend, located in Clifftown Road, just outside Southend station. I lost count of the times I travelled there, again walking to Chalkwell station and then catching the train and making my way across the road to Essex Radio. We used to have discussions as well, which went out live. I can remember on the panel one day was Tony Newton, then just an MP, later to become the Minister of Social Security who appointed me as a member of the Access Committee for England.

For five years I wrote a daily bulletin for all disabled people. My mum used to help me with these, as I had to have books and catalogues read to me so that I could write down the information I wanted to pass on.

Eventually the BBC opened BBC Essex, based in Chelmsford but with a studio in Westcliff, not far from where I live. However, most of my interviews are done at home or over the telephone.

Local broadcasting is so important for blind people. I depend on it for my news each day, for the weather forecast and, when I am away at Point Clear (I'll tell you more about that later) for the time and height of the tide, as my bungalow is right on the sea wall and I certainly need to know the high tides. I also enjoy listening to the football commentaries on BBC Essex and Radio

Five Live. I have supported Southend football team ever since my friend Pam's brother, Tony Ruark, who lived next door to me, played for Southend Reserves in the late fifties. One of the first campaigns I was involved in was getting an audio description for the football matches at Roots Hall stadium, the home of Southend United. Toc H had provided the audio system for Southend Hospital, and we were able to get that installed at Roots Hall. This was in the late sixties, so it must have been one of the first audio-described services in the country.

I have learnt so much from the radio, and this is why I like to pass on information to other blind people, as well as educate the general public about the way they can help blind people.

I have taken part in dozens of live and recorded radio and television news programmes over the years. When I went to Australia for the World Blind Union conference I even ended up on one of their radio stations. Another media appearance abroad was while I was in Sicily at one of my European Blind Union meetings, when we all ended up on their main live Saturday night television show and I talked about pavements and guide dogs. In Sicily motorbikes drive not only on the pavements but also through the shop doors!

One of the most nerve-wracking broadcasts I ever had to do was for the Radio 4 live Sunday morning service, which came from Westcliff Baptist Church. I had to read one of the lessons in Braille. Although I can give talks even without notes, I am not a good Braille reader and I found that experience very hard. My friend Alan played the organ, and David Scott Blackhall, who used to present the In Touch programme, did the sermon. So three of those taking part were totally blind.

And one of the most interesting programmes I did was with John Hayes, when he did a kind of Desert Island Discs with me and I talked about my life and chose my favourite records. It made a change from all the campaigning topics that I normally discuss. Another interesting broadcast with BBC Essex was when I was Steve Scruton's guest on the Tea at Three programme. I made him a sponge cake and spoke about my life and the work of the Federation.

My first time on the Today programme on Radio 4 was in 1976, when I was trying to get access for guide dogs into the Chelsea Flower Show. Lord Snowdon phoned me at home to tell me that he had written an article about this problem in The Times and that I should try to get as much publicity as possible. Naturally, I was very nervous about going on such a programme. The minister at my church, who did a lot of broadcasting, told me to imagine that I was just talking to one person standing at their sink, washing up, and not think of the six million people who were also listening. I have always thought of that, and it does help.

Following that broadcast I was contacted by the BBC television programme, Nationwide. Reporters spent three days with me and then put out an 18-minute story about me. After this, Mary Parkinson contacted me and invited me onto her 25-minute Good Afternoon programme. Although the Nationwide feature essentially focused on my various campaigns relating to access for guide dogs, it also showed me pouring out a cup of tea using the liquid level indicator. After the programme the BBC received around 3,000 telephone calls asking where they could buy this gadget. The RNIB then took it on board. Ironically, every time I went into their shop in Great Portland Street to ask for one they were always out of stock - they simply could not keep up with demand.

I was giving a talk in an old people's home one day, demonstrating this aid, when one of the elderly residents said that she could do with one of these gadgets to help pour out her gin and tonic. The warden, not to mention the other residents, was rather surprised, to say the least, that this lady had gin and tonic in her room!

Now 33 years later, this is still the most popular item sold. In fact John Godber, the Products Manager at the RNIB, will tell you that 100 people go blind every day and 90 liquid level indicators are sold daily. This proves that blind people know what they want and need.

In those days, if you wanted to look at a product in the RNIB shop you had to ask and the item would be brought to the counter. I kept asking if the range of products kept in stock could be put on display. At the same time a member of the Federation, Martin Milligan, had drawn up a document recommending a resource centre. The first one was opened in Glasgow, and eventually we persuaded the RNIB to open one in Great Portland Street. These resource centres are now established all over the country.

I have always said that the hardest thing for blind people is to find out what aids are available. This is why I try to give as much information as I can by contributing to tape magazines and, for the past few years, I have produced two national tape magazines: Fed Talk, for members of the NFB; and Mobility Matters, issued monthly and covering all aspects of mobility, access and transport, and one of a series of tapes produced by Living Without Sight Ltd based in Wigan.

So, one day a month I turn one of my desks in my office into a recording studio. My office is our third bedroom, kitted out with three desks, a Braille machine, a radio cassette player, a talking scanner, a CD player, two telephones and, for the past two years, a talking laptop computer.

One of my desks is for the helpers that come in to read to me. Moira has been coming since 1986, usually on a Monday morning. She will write my birthday and Christmas cards for me and help with all those many jobs that need to be written, such as bills and form filling. My neighbour Lily used to come over every evening to do other reading, but for the last year, since she had a long stay in hospital, I have been going round to her house some evenings. For the past five years we have cooked Lily her dinner and since her discharge from hospital Alvin has taken her meal round to her house every day, at about 6 o'clock. It is no trouble to cook for three instead of two.

Ever since 1991 Lily has completed most of my expenses claims, which is very important. The majority of the work I do is voluntary, but I do spend a lot of money on train and taxi fares. I have to be very organised and keep these receipts in a separate part of my purse, as they are just pieces of card and paper with nothing tactile on them. Without these receipts I cannot claim my expenses. Filling in claim forms is a very long and tiring job, as each organisation I work for has different kinds of forms.

Without the help and support of my friends and helpers, I could not have done all the voluntary work I have done over the past years and I am extremely grateful for everything they have done for me.

CHAPTER 7 – LEARNING THROUGH BRAILLE AND TOUCH

Jacqueline started school in September 1969, and around that time a new daily newspaper was launched, called the Evening Echo. I was really pleased when they included an article on the cost of school uniforms, and Jacqueline was chosen to have her photograph in the new newspaper in her full kit. Nobody knew she was my daughter, so she appeared in the paper in her own right rather than through any connection with me.

Jacqueline's first day at Chalkwell School was a big day in her life, and I was so pleased that my friend Jill came round to walk to the school with us. Although it was only a five-minute walk there were three roads to cross, so I was able to pass on to Jacqueline what I had been taught about road safety in the GLB. I still had no confidence to go anywhere else on my own, however - not even to the shops at the top of my road.

While Jacqueline was at school Mr Denny gave me my long cane training. The first part of the course was to train Mick how to guide me properly, and this made it so much easier to get around, especially walking in and out of doors and up and down steps. Even now people will say, "Steps coming up," when it's a flight of steps going down. It is no good saying to me that there is a chair "over there", because I do not know where it is. You need to put my hand on the back of the chair and tell me if it is a high or low one, whether it has arms, and also which way it is facing. I would also need to know if there is a table in front of it and if it is a high or low table.

I have also found many times that people will ask a person accompanying me, "Does she take sugar in her tea?" instead of asking me directly. People seemed to think that because I was blind I could not do many normal activities; in fact, I did not think myself that I would be able to dance again, cook or run a GLB company. I had never met a blind person before I went blind, and had never been spoken to by a blind person at school, so I really did not know what I would be able to do. I was not offered any rehabilitation training, even when the home teacher came to visit me. All I did was find out as I went along.

It was when Jacqueline was about three that I discovered how useful learning Braille might be for me. A lady called Betty, whom I met at a church function, told me that Braille knitting books and cookery books, as well as Braille tape measures, were available, which would have been so useful to me over the previous four years. I still did not know about all the gadgets that were made by the RNIB.

A lady from Crowstone Church offered to come and sit with Jacqueline while I had my Braille lessons each week. It was a very slow learning process for me and I have never been very good at it, but at least I can keep my diary and all my telephone numbers in Braille. I find it helpful to have tins of food labelled in Braille and my cooker and washing machine controls marked. My Braille lessons were rather hit and miss. The first teacher started me with reading Braille, but then moved away. The next teacher decided to teach me to write Braille first, and then a couple of weeks later got another girl, who had also gone blind and was good at Braille, to come over and teach me to read, but she too moved away. I had to teach myself after that. I wanted to be able to read Jacqueline stories, but I think she learnt to read quicker than I did.

When Betty had come to visit me to tell me about the Braille knitting books she was accompanied by her guide dog, Jack. This was my first encounter with a guide dog, and I was amazed that they had walked all the way from her home, which was about 20 minutes away, and found my house. Seeds were gradually being sown in my head that one day I would have a guide dog.

Because of the attitude of sighted people to my blindness and also the lack of information, when Jill Welsh asked me if I would talk to her Sunday School class about how I use my hands I jumped at the chance. Her daughter, Sally, was four at the time and Jacqueline was three. I can remember taking the poodle I had knitted and a face that I had made for the GLB girls to teach them how to do up buttons and zips and other activities. Because Jill was also a schoolteacher, I then started to give talks at schools, church groups, etc. In fact, over the years I have given more than 800 talks and raised thousands of pounds for different charities.

When I give my talks I share my experiences of what I had to do and learn when I went totally blind. When you can see you tend to take for granted seemingly simple, everyday activities, but for a blind person these are much more complicated. You would think that getting washed and dressed is easy, but there are so many things to take into consideration. For instance, first of all you have to work out which tap is hot and which is cold. We used to have raised letters on the taps in our bathroom, but when we replaced our bathroom suite we were told that they simply weren't made anymore. So you run your water and then hope that no one else has moved the soap. Now you want to clean your teeth and you find your toothbrush – easy! You locate the toothpaste, squeeze it on your brush and start to brush your teeth ... So what is that horrible taste?! In my case, I had used Mick's hair cream instead of toothpaste, because the tubes and the tops were identical. I soon learnt I had a nose, and I had to use it to smell such items so that I knew what I was using.

Knowing whether it is day or night is a problem that I found very frustrating, and I often would phone someone to ask if it was dark so I knew whether or not to put the lights on in my house. In recent years I found out from my friend Peter, who has been totally blind from birth, that there is a gadget that indicates the presence of light with a bleeping sound. Although a light is of no help to me, my guide dogs need it as well as any visitors to the house.

One of the first things I missed was being able to see the colour of my clothes. This was helped when John Slade invented a colour code for games, and in a conversation with him I suggested that this idea would be good for marking my clothes. John then created a series of buttons that followed his colour coding. These buttons were produced even before his games, and of all the aids I have I find these the most useful. If you sew these onto your clothes you can identify the colour of the garment by feeling their shape. For example, white is round, black is square, a cross is red and a star is blue. These buttons can be used for marking other items, such as sheets, towels or even shoe polish.

Being blind will make you more tidy and organised, so you know exactly where things are. Catering for 2,000 people and dealing with large quantities when I worked at Shell meant that we had to work tidily and systematically, and my experiences there were good training for me.

When children ask me what it is like being blind, I tell them it is very tiring as you are always concentrating. It makes you become very nosey, as you are always listening to what is going on around you. I always have a radio on when I am in a room, as it is a good location aid. Although I can pick the post up off the mat every morning, I still miss being able to read it and have had to rely on others to read any printed material to me.

In the absence of any form of rehabilitation, I had to teach myself how to cope with running my home and looking after Jacqueline. It was not easy, but with Mick's help and that of my friends I seemed to get everything done without any major incidents. The accidents I did have were usually funny. For instance, I mistook pearl barley for rice and made a pearl barley pudding and once sprayed the room with oven cleaner instead of air freshener, both due to the fact that they were identical to the touch. Eventually I was invited to be a member of the British Standards Institute committee, which looked into the marking of containers to ensure that all poisonous substances were easily identifiable. For example, on a bleach bottle you can read in Braille the word 'Bleach', or 'Thick Bleach'. However, when this labelling system was first introduced, although dangerous substances would have 'Do Not Drink' in Braille on the bottle, it still did not tell you exactly what the bottle contained. On some bottles you will also find fluting, or raised lines, to indicate a poisonous substance. However, there are still hundreds of products, such as tins of food and packets of other commodities that feel identical. For instance, I know of one blind person who could not distinguish between a packet of weed killer and a packet of custard powder. Over the six years that I attended these meetings, I would often take with me two products that I used regularly and were identical in shape and size; for example, a tin of furniture polish and a tin of hair spray. This was one good reason why I learnt Braille and can label such tins. However, the vast majority of blind people do not learn Braille and, therefore, have a real problem in identifying tins, cans and packages.

One of the things I miss doing most of all is shopping for clothes on my own. I know many shops will provide helpful assistants to take you around the shop, but it is not the same as shopping for yourself. In the last few years I have bought a lot of clothes from catalogues, which are delivered to my home, so my friends Moira and Lily can then assist me. As I am small and need short fittings, this is a good way of ensuring that I buy clothes that will fit me. My daughter Jacqueline will take me shopping in her area when I visit her in Rownhams, near Southampton. I like going with her, as she shows me all the modern fashions and is very good at describing the colours by relating them to things I can remember, such as sky blue, green grass, lemons, etc.

Since having guide dogs I have bought clothes to fit around my dogs and to ensure that I can be seen by traffic. For example, when I had two yellow Labrador dogs I could never wear black, navy or brown suits, trousers or dresses, as any dog hairs would be too visible. Likewise, when I had my four black dogs I could not wear very light colours. So that the traffic can see me I try to wear brightly coloured jackets and coats. I do not know why manufacturers make outdoor coats in such dark colours. I also wear light and bright colours when dancing, so that Alvin can see where I am. His sight is not very good and he finds it difficult on the dance floor when people are wearing grey and similar colours. My friend Moira sews the shaped buttons onto my clothes for me. I do not have buttons on my white underwear, as it can be uncomfortable, but I do have them on black underwear, as I would not want to wear a black bra under a white blouse. I do love clothes and I have far too many, but I wear clean clothes every day, and because I do so much travelling I need clothes that will not crease and that are appropriate for the occasion.

Although I do wear hats I have to be careful if it is windy, as if my hat blew off I would not be able to retrieve it, so in the winter I wear hats with ties or a scarf attached. Although I like to wear gloves in winter too, they are one thing I will never give as a present, as I am very superstitious and they mean 'a parting'. My dad used to sell ladies' and girls' shoes, so when he was alive he kept me well supplied with footwear. Because I do a lot of walking I normally wear flat, comfortable shoes. Since 1985 I have been buying my shoes in Majorca, as I have found some there that are ideal – fur-lined and very cheap and comfortable. In the winter I wear boots that are fur-lined and have no laces. Although I do like slingback shoes, it would not be safe to wear these while travelling – I once lost such a shoe when getting onto a train. I also like shopping when I am on holiday, especially shops selling bags in Majorca.

In the past few years I have bought cases that are on wheels and have a solid handle that I can pull. With a guide dog on a lead in one hand and my trolley in the other, it can prove very difficult negotiating flights of stairs at railway stations, etc., and it can require assistance from staff, who tend to be very few and far between. I also have my name strapped around my case so that other people can recognise it.

Coping with blindness is a learning process and these are just some of the practicalities of daily living and potential hazards around the home that maybe a sighted person would not even think about. It was after gaining my independence with my first guide dog that wider issues outside the home became more apparent and led to my campaigning years.

CHAPTER 8 – GUIDE DOGS

Although I had received my mobility training and was taking Jacqueline to school, I really did not have much confidence and would not go to any of the shops on my own. I had heard about guide dogs and had seen a film at my church - strangely enough, it was called Leading Lady, and Lady was the name of my fifth guide dog. There were many reasons why I did not have a guide dog until 1970. The main stumbling block was that I did not want to go to Leamington Spa, about 200 miles away, for the required four weeks' training, as this would mean leaving Jacqueline for a long time. Another factor was that I knew there were many places that would not allow guide dogs. I had even been told by a social worker for the blind that it was not easy for blind people to get jobs if they had a guide dog. So I had no encouragement from anyone except my GLB girls.

I finally decided to take the plunge on my 31st birthday. I was at home all day apart from taking Jacqueline to school. My dad made his usual daily phone call from work and asked me if my mum had been round, but she had not visited. I found out that she had been to the theatre, which was only a five-minute bus ride away. She did not come to see me at all that day and this really depressed me. So I made my mind up there and then that I would go out when I wanted and, of course, would take Jacqueline out as well on my own.

I applied to the Guide Dogs for the Blind Association and, after a visit from a trainer, I was called to go for training in October 1971. Mick drove me to the Leamington Spa training centre and left me there, feeling very nervous and worrying about Jacqueline. It had been arranged for one of our neighbours, Mrs Marlow, to take her to school each morning, as Mick had to leave for work much earlier than the start of her school day.

After settling down at the centre and getting acquainted with the other ten students on my training course, I met trainer Lee Mitchell. On the Saturday we were taken for walks around the grounds and then for what seemed like a long walk into Leamington Spa town centre. After lunch on the following afternoon we congregated in the lounge and were given our equipment - lead, collar, harness, etc., and each student was told the name and breed of the dog that had been allocated to them. Mine was a black Labrador called Topsy. We then retired to our bedrooms to await the arrival of the trainer with our dogs. This was a very happy moment in my life. It was the first dog I'd had since my pet Sally had died when I was eight years old.

Mick and Jacqueline came to visit me the following Sunday, and when they first saw me out walking with Topsy they commented that she even had my wobble, as the centre matched up as closely as possible each dog with its new owner. I qualified as a guide dog owner on 11th November, a date that had particular significance. Not only was it Remembrance Day, but also it was my grandmother's birthday - my mother's mum, whom I had never met.

I was told that Topsy had been puppy-walked in Enfield by a London taxi driver called Laddy Rodgers. They had a daughter who was in the Girls' Brigade, so Topsy had been used to church and young children. It was really strange that Topsy had come from Enfield, the home of my grandparents and their relatives. All the other dogs had been puppy-walked in the Birmingham area. My granddad had always said that he wanted a little black girl called Topsy, so of course my grandmother, who was still alive, was thrilled that I had been given this particular dog.

The four-week training course was very intensive and taught me a lot about the health and care of my guide dog. The training began with walking the dog in harness while accompanied by the trainer, so Lee Mitchell had a lead clipped onto Topsy's collar and walked quietly on the other side of her. All of a sudden, after a ten-minute walk, I stopped at a kerb and was really surprised to hear from Lee that I had been walking on my own for the last five minutes. Lee had unclipped his lead without my knowing. It was November, with conkers and leaves on the ground, and I was just amazed that Topsy was able to guide me round all the various obstacles.

Before we left the training centre my trainer told Jacqueline, who was still only six years old, that she should not treat Topsy like a pet and that when Topsy was in her bed she should not touch her or talk to her, as this is a space where the dog knows it can go for a bit of peace in a noisy and busy household. Mick brought us home by car, but I had done some training on buses and trains.

Getting Topsy in November 1971 was a real turning point and changed my life completely, giving me back all the independence that I had lost when I went blind.

Although she was an excellent guide dog, she did have her naughty moments. One Christmas Jacqueline had saved up to buy her dad a box of sweets. It was a few days before Christmas Day and all the presents had been wrapped and placed in a box next to the Christmas tree. Mick had taken Jacqueline and me to a carol service at the church, and when we got back home we were greeted by an unwelcome sight. Topsy had found the box of sweets and had eaten the lot, leaving the floor strewn with wrappers. As you can imagine, Jacqueline was heartbroken. It taught us all a lesson: guide dogs are no different from any other dog (or cats, for that matter) when it comes to their stomach, and you should never leave any kind of food within reach.

Unfortunately, a dog's life is relatively short and, 38 years later, I have my sixth guide dog, Amanda. Losing your guide dog is traumatic, and as I have got older I have learnt to appreciate every day I have with my dog.

Topsy ended up working with me for 12 years, until she had to be put to sleep. I was shopping in Southend with my mum, when Topsy just lay down on the ground and could not get up, so we got a taxi and took her straight to the vet's. Our vet, Mr Downs, examined her, gave her an injection and took some tests.

Topsy seemed to recover from this episode, but the following week I had to go back for the test results. This was the moment I had dreaded. I was told that Topsy had terminal cancer of the glands. Mr Downs said that she had between one to eighteen months left, but in fact she only lived for a further three weeks.

We had gone out one afternoon for our normal walk to the park. She found my seat and I put on her play collar, which had a bell on it so I could tell where she was. Usually she would be off for a romp, but on this day she just sat there. Then after about ten minutes she just stood up and wanted to go home. A little while later I fed her, and then she just went and lay down in the hall. She never got up again. After an hour I phoned my vet. Unfortunately, Mr Downs had gone on holiday, but a very nice Mr Hepworth arrived. After a very long chat, we decided that she should be put to sleep. There was a possibility of an operation, but this could have caused her more suffering and I did not want that.

All her life she had worked as well as she had on that first day - stopping at all roads, checking for traffic and not bumping me in to anything. As you can imagine, to lose her like this just broke my heart.

My husband dug a deep hole so that we could bury her in the garden and wrapped her in a blanket, which had been made for her by one of the girls at Bullwood Hall, a girls' borstal that I had been visiting for two years.

I had to wait 12 weeks for another guide dog. This was a terrible time. Not only was I trying to get over the shock of Topsy going so quickly, but also it was like stepping back to the time before I had Topsy. I just had no confidence to go out on my own and had to depend on my family and friends to go with me.

It was July 1980 when I travelled the 200 miles to Leamington Spa once again to train with my new dog, Bunty. She was a very light yellow Labrador, a lot larger than Topsy, and was only 17 months old.

Well, I could write a whole book about Bunty, but, to cut a very long story short, I only had her for six months. At the end of this period, the manager of the training centre decided that they had given me the wrong dog. I had become a physical and mental wreck. I was physically exhausted because Bunty pulled me all the time, and it was a mental strain as Topsy had been so well behaved at all times and in all places. This was at the height of my access campaigning, so to have a guide dog that was not well behaved was an embarrassment. For instance, I was doing a Channel Four pre-recorded interview about access when I found Bunty chewing the cable under my chair!

I returned to Leamington for another week's retraining with her that December, in case it was me that was doing something wrong. Bunty was retrained and was allocated to a man who could cope with her strength. Naturally I was very upset, and I was also cross that I had been given a dog that was unsuitable. I brought Bunty back home with me while I waited for my next dog.

It was only a couple of weeks before I returned to Leamington Spa to be trained with my third dog, Brandy. She was a little golden Labrador and was too good to be true.

The new partnership was working very well, just like it did with Topsy, and I was returning to good health again. However, the first time I went to the RNIB building in Great Portland Street in London, I was stepping out of a lift when another guide dog went for Brandy. From that day on, whenever she saw another dog she would, for a split second, forget her work and adopt defensive mode, and would try to go for the other dog.

I worked with Brandy for three-and-a-half years, and although I did not have any accidents I had a lot of near misses. Brandy was the most affectionate dog I have had, and she comforted me through the time of my divorce. I was so pleased when my publisher chose the picture of Brandy and me for the front cover of this book.

The Guide Dogs Association took Brandy back to Redbridge, to a new training centre, for some tests while my mother took me to Guernsey for a two-week holiday. On my return, my trainer told me that Brandy would have to be retired and I would not be able to keep her. It was thought that she might upset my next guide dog and so, with great sorrow, she went to live back in the Midlands, where she had been puppy-walked. Brandy's trainer was Mark Fisher, who was working at the Guide Dog School in Melbourne when I went to Australia for the World Blind Union conference.

In August 1986 I went to Redbridge Training Centre to be trained with my fourth guide dog, Quella, a beautiful black Labrador. She, like Topsy, was the perfect guide dog. She never let me down and we had no accidents. She was trained by Pete Smith and was by my side when I married my second husband, Alvin, in 1987. Pete was late arriving at the church, and as I walked up the aisle Quella was wagging her tail as she had seen Pete at the door.

Alvin also had a guide dog at that time. His dog was a yellow curly-coated retriever called Otis. When the two dogs were together they were very well behaved. It was quite funny, as people just used to ask us how the dogs got on together, and never how Alvin and I got on!

Quella worked until she was 11, when she was retired. Having been parted from Brandy I wanted to keep Quella, and she remained with me until she was put to sleep at the age of 15½.

I was trained with my fifth guide dog, Lady, in June 1996, so for four years I had two dogs. Alvin, by this time was with his sixth dog, a black Labrador retriever cross called Fabian. A month after Quella died Fabian, aged 11, was diagnosed with cancer and had to be put to sleep. Poor Lady really missed them both.

My Lady was another perfect guide dog. She, like Topsy and Quella, gave me so much confidence, and when her arthritis started at the age of only 9 I was very upset. However, with a good vet and modern treatment she was able to carry on working until she was 11. She was eventually put to sleep, at the age of 13½, while lying on the floor in our lounge. A tumour on her leg had been operated on twice, but the disease had finally spread into her bloodstream.

As a result of Lady's bad legs, my walking had been very limited over those last four years and I had put on quite a bit of weight. I was coming up to my 65th birthday, and weighing twelve stone six at a height of only four foot eleven inches was too much. My clothes size had gone up to a size 18. I have talking weighing scales, and I thought perhaps they had stopped functioning correctly, but their reading was confirmed when I visited Jacqueline and she weighed me on her scales. Over the next 18 months I lost three stone and got down to a size 12, and I have maintained that weight and size to date. I feel so much better for losing the weight.

It was a good job that I was fit and healthy when I was given my sixth guide dog, Amanda, in September 2005. She was a very lively black Labrador, aged almost two.

Since I had undergone training with my last guide dog, Lady, all the training centres had closed and new kinds of training had been introduced. I had to be trained from home, which was good from the point of view that I knew my own area, but I missed the training that I had received at Leamington Spa and Redbridge training centres with my other five dogs.

After four years with Amanda, she is now a good guide dog, but the first two years were hard work. Without Alvin's help and my fitness, I don't think I could have coped.

Instead of the dogs living in a training centre while in training, they live with boarders. Les and Pat, who were Amanda's boarders, have looked after her sometimes when I have been on trips abroad and was unable to take her with me. They now live in St Leonards and meet up with us when we go to Eastbourne for the sixties weekends.

I still keep in touch with my puppy-walkers. These are the kind people who look after the puppies from the age of six weeks until they go for their training at about a year old. I have also met the lady who bred Amanda, when I was in Scarborough in 2008 for a conference. Ann Townsend and her husband had still got Amanda's mother, Kate, and her grandmother, Quiz. It was lovely to meet them, and we have a photo of the three dogs together.

Without these people, whether breeders, boarders or puppy-walkers, we would not be able to have our guide dogs. They all give up so much time and love to our dogs, and it must be as hard for them to give them over for training as it is for us when we lose them, whether as a result of not being the right match, through changes in family circumstances or when they die. A dog's life is very short really, and as I have got older I have learnt to appreciate every day I have with my dog.

My Lady was one of the first guide dogs to have a passport, and she went with me to Majorca to stay with our neighbours, Alison and Gordon, who have a villa high up in the mountains. Amanda has now been on holiday every year with us. She watches me get her bag ready for the flight. I weigh out her food for the two weeks and pack her blanket, toy, and brush and comb. We always use the same bag, so she knows that it is hers. It has her name strap round it, so the airport staff know that the bag belongs to a guide dog.

A couple of years ago we were checking in at Heathrow airport and I was talking to the girl on the desk, while Alvin was on my right-hand side, putting the cases on the conveyer. Amanda, who was on my left, must have seen her bag disappearing and she pushed in front of me and jumped up after her bag. Although I was cross with her, it caused everyone to stop work and have a good laugh.

When we arrive at Palma airport, Amanda is always watching for the cases and her bag to come round on the conveyor. We are usually met by my friend Jill, who lives in Majorca and picks us up in her car. We always know when she is coming, as Amanda's tail starts going into high-speed action.

When we arrive at the hotel Amanda knows exactly where we are, and while Alvin gets the cases out we are straight off into the hotel and heading for the reception desk. The manager of the Carla Blanca says that Amanda is the best-behaved guest he has. The hotel has a porter on the door, and every time we go in and out we hear, "Good morning, Amanda" or "Good night, Amanda". Alvin and I are not treated to any such greetings, and we find it quite funny.

CHAPTER 9 – INDEPENDENCE AND NEW OBSTACLES

I had only been at home for a week with my first guide dog, Topsy, when my first battle regarding access started. I was thrilled to have Topsy and that I would be able to take Jacqueline out on my own, so the first place we went to was the local library. I never imagined that there would be any problem, so we just entered the library, handed in our old books and went to the children's section so that Jacqueline could pick some new books. We had only been there a couple of minutes when I was approached by a lady who asked whether I would mind waiting outside with my dog and she would help Jacqueline choose her books. I just could not believe what I was hearing. It not only upset me but Jacqueline as well. She started to cry, as she did not want me to leave her and, of course, I had no intention of doing so. As a result, we both went home without our books.

This experience really affected me deeply, and I shall never forget that moment when the lady spoke to me. This was the first time since I had lost my sight that I had gone somewhere on my own with Jacqueline, and I had been refused access with my guide dog. Fortunately, Barbara Bridge, a friend whom I had met in hospital when Jacqueline was born, knew someone that worked for the Council and was responsible for the library service. He said that I would be allowed into the library next time, but when Mick went into the library and mentioned to the staff about my going in there again their response was, "We have got to let her in." I never did go back to that library and the whole experience made Jacqueline think that every time we went anywhere the same thing would happen again. Unfortunately it often did, and this is why I have campaigned from that day on for better access, not only for my benefit but also for my family as well as all the other guide dog owners and their families. However, I was allowed into my local Palace Theatre, and eventually the Cliffs Pavilion when it was built.

At that time there were many restaurants that would not allow guide dogs, not to mention certain shops. Keddies, a large store in Southend, would not accept guide dogs, and I was warned by someone at church even before I went for my training that I would not be allowed access at Dixons, another large store that I had frequented for many years. In addition, in the past we had been to Butlin's and Pontin's holiday camps, but now that I had Topsy they would not allow me to stay there. It took 11 years of writing to them before they changed their policy. These attitudes made me very cross. If I had not had the real incentive to be independent I might never have decided to get a guide dog. I did not want Jacqueline to grow up thinking that she would have to guide me and look after me as she grew up.

I thought that starting to travel once again with my new guide dog Topsy would not be too difficult. I had used Fenchurch Street station for seven years when I worked in the City as a cook. Although that was seven years earlier, I could still remember the layout of the station. So the first time I went with Topsy I got off the train and walked towards the gates. I was telling her to walk straight on, but what I had not realised was that she had gone through the gates without my knowing. The next thing I knew was hearing one man say to another, "Are you going to tell her, or shall I?" I then guessed what had happened: Topsy had walked straight into the men's toilets. I just said, "I can smell where I am, thank you"! If I had realised that we had already passed through the gates I would have told Topsy to find the steps. It's a story that makes the children laugh when I give my talks.

When I came home with Topsy I started to take Jacqueline to school. It was only a three-minute walk, but there were three roads to cross. The third was right outside the school and involved negotiating a zebra crossing, so we had to be very careful.

Once I had taken Jacqueline to the school gate I would meet up with two other mums, Jean and Renie, who also had dogs. So once we got into Chalkwell Park we would let the dogs off their leads so that they could play together. I would hold either Jean or Renie's arm and we would walk right round the park, so Topsy got a good run. We did that every day until our children moved on to senior school.

Jean and Renie both moved to other parts of the district. Renie sadly died a couple of years ago, but I still see Jean at the Chalkwell Methodist ladies' club when I have the time to go.

I used to go and meet Jacqueline at lunchtime and bring her home for dinner most days, and I would always then give Topsy a long walk and usually went round to visit a friend. It was so nice to be able to go out every day rather than be confined to the house and reliant on someone else coming to take me out, which had been the case for seven years.

Mind you, I was never bored at home. I always had my radio on and would always have some knitting on the go, and for six months I would be working on the carnival floats. I also had my washing and ironing to do and, of course, my cooking. Although I had been a cook, preparing meals is very different when you are blind. I realised that I would have to weigh ingredients on the old-fashioned type of scales that uses weights, and Mick had to travel all the way to Wickford in order to find the right type. Although nowadays you can buy talking scales, I still prefer to use my original ones. Until I learnt Braille, I had to keep tins of food in the cupboards in alphabetical order, and as our kitchen was only eight foot square I had to keep it very tidy.

Another mum who used to walk to the school sometimes was Sue Foster. If I was unwell she would pick Jacqueline up on the way past my gate. One day there was a thick fog and she called round and said, "I think you had better take the children today." I think all the children started to consider what it was like for me to be blind when they were unable to see through that fog. Another example would be the day we had a power cut. Jacqueline was about seven and I was bathing her when all the lights went out. As I cannot see light at all I did not know what had happened, but Jacqueline started to cry and wanted me to stop bathing her, and my husband, who was downstairs doing the washing-up, abandoned what he was doing, rushed up the stairs and said, "Where are the candles?" I know my friend Jill said to her children, "Now you know what it's like for Auntie Jill all the time."

The two years that I'd had to take Jacqueline to school just using my white cane were such a mental strain. But when I had Topsy to guide me I was so much more relaxed, and could depend on her to guide me round all those obstacles on the pavements that I'd had to try to negotiate with my white cane.

The public could make life so much easier for blind people if only they had a little thought: doing things that don't cost a penny, such as cutting back their overhanging branches. A wet, leafy twig or prickly branch can be very frightening when it hits you in the face. Also, people just drive onto the pavement without thinking what a hazard they might be causing. Apart from the fact that they might be blocking the footpath and causing pedestrians to step into the road to get past it, they can also crack and break the pavement, which leads to people tripping and falling. My husband Alvin's mother had such a fall and it led to her death. She was visiting her brother, who had recently been discharged from hospital, when she tripped and fell on a broken pavement outside his home in Romford. The damage had been caused by a lorry continually parking there, despite many complaints to the police. Alvin's mum spent two years in hospital and ultimately died from her injuries. The Council paid insurance money to the family, but her seven sons and eleven grandchildren would rather have had their mother and grandmother than the money.

In my own road we have a grass verge that people often park on, making it very difficult to cross the road. The cars churn up the grass, and when it's wet it can cause you to slip. Pavements and grass verges were not built to accommodate vehicles, and in addition to the hazards already mentioned they can damage gas and electricity pipes and equipment buried under the ground.

Even though it is illegal to cycle on the pavement, people still do, even adults. When I was young and cycled a lot I would never have dreamt of riding my bike on the pavement. If the road got too busy, particularly when I heard the petrol tankers that used to drive through Benfleet to get to Canvey Island coming up behind me, I would just stop, get off my bike and walk. Cyclists nowadays don't think that they should ever stop, and this is why they ride on the pavement and even cycle through traffic lights when they are red.

One of our long-running Federation campaigns is for cycle

tracks to be built. Local authorities continue to install dangerous dual-use footways and footpaths with just a white line down the middle to separate pedestrians from cyclists. This gives no safe place for blind people to walk, as we cannot see the white line. Cyclists should be on road space and not on pedestrian space. In our Federation leaflet we convey an important message to cyclists: blind people can't see you, deaf and hard-of-hearing people can't hear you, and elderly and disabled people can't move out of the way.

In the past, all bikes were fitted with a bell and there was a requirement to use it. But in the seventies the Pedestrians' Association persuaded the Government to remove this requirement. I was furious, as there had been no prior consultation, and when I became a Federation representative member of this association I fought very hard to get this requirement reinstated. I even bought the Minister at the time, Peter Bottomley, a bell as a Christmas present!

Although it is a requirement for all new bikes to be fitted with bells, there is still no requirement to use it, and I can remember buying my grandson Joseph his first bike when he was four years old and being horrified to find out that it had no bell and I had to buy one as an extra.

I can fully understand why children have to ride their bikes on the pavements, but they should still be taught to stop when they see a pedestrian coming rather than whiz round them and frighten people. They should also learn not to leave their bikes lying on the pavement when they have finished playing with them, and instead put them back in their gardens or at least take them off the footpath.

My early experiences of coping with blindness, as well as the access issues I experienced with my first guide dog, stood me in good stead for the campaigning years to come.

CHAPTER 10 – ACCESS, DISABILITY AND MOBILITY

During the Spring of 1970 I received two telephone calls that would change my life completely. One was from Tom Parker, secretary of the National League of the Blind and Disabled, and the other was from Stan Bell, public relations officer for the NFB. Both organisations were setting up new branches in Essex, and as they had heard me on the radio and knew that I lived in Essex they thought I might like to join these. Stan asked me if I would go to a meeting in Southend even before I joined the Federation. The first Access Committee was formed and they wanted a representative from the Federation, so you might say I was dropped in it rather quickly, and little did I know what I had let myself in for.

When I joined the Southend Access Committee, it was the first one of its kind in the country. The committee was comprised of people with different kinds of disabilities and council officers and was chaired by a local councillor. One officer was the Southend Borough engineer, with whom we had many differences of opinion.

Our first aim was to enable access to the local swimming pool, and this took about three years to achieve. The council then wanted to pedestrianise the high street and we fought really hard against these plans, as we knew that it would prevent many elderly and disabled people from getting to the shops in the high street due to a lack of access for buses. Remember, in those days very few people had cars and there were no out-of-town shops. The response was always the same: we were only a minority group and therefore our needs could not really be considered. I attended that meeting every month for about ten years and learnt a great deal about the needs of people with disabilities and also the attitude of able-bodied people towards those of us who were blind or in wheelchairs.

It was during that time that I became concerned about kerbs

being flattened to make it easier for wheelchair users to cross roads, as this could create a danger for blind people because they would not be able to tell whether they were on the pavement or in the road. We also started a dial-a-ride service so that people with disabilities who wanted to go swimming or take part in other activities could be picked up from their homes and taken direct to the venue. This service still operates, but it is still not able to cover the large area adequately or operate for the number of hours needed.

Although the Civic Centre, which was the council building where we met, was quite accessible in those days, today it is way behind the current standards.

It must have been September before I went to my first Federation meeting, held at Gidea Park. The branch was called The Essex and Metropolitan and I attended the meetings there until 1974, when I formed the South East Essex branch. Our meetings were held monthly in the local church hall. We attempted to establish a branch of the League too, in Southend, but it did not get off the ground and so I stayed with the Federation.

It was also in 1974 that I first met Peg and Dick Gargan. Dick was a member of the Liberal Party, led at that time by David Steel, and he suggested I should join and maybe one day stand for the Council.

Well, I did join, and I have been a member ever since. I was invited to speak at the autumn conference in Llandudno in 1978 about our Give Us Back Our Pavement campaign, which had been launched in June that year by the NFB. I have spoken at most party conferences since then as a delegate for Southend West. I even had the opportunity to speak in the merger debate at Blackpool, when the Liberal Party joined up with the Social Democratic Party. Many of my contributions at the conferences have been shown on television.

I stood for Southend Council twice during the seventies. It was a time when the Liberals were not doing very well and I was up against the current deputy Mayor, but I still got good support and was only 200 votes behind. I gave up my Girls' Brigade work and my old-time dancing to do this, so that I could concentrate on canvassing. I canvassed every street in the ward and got to meet a lot of people. I was also busy giving my talks to schools and other groups, amounting to about 50 a year, and attending around 100 committee meetings a year both in London and at home, so I simply could not fit in anything else.

For the past two years the Liberal Party conference has been held in Bournemouth, so I was able to stay with my daughter in Rownhams and travel each day by train and taxi, of course accompanied by my guide dog Amanda. It is always difficult to attend such conferences on your own, but it is not always easy to find someone to go with you.

I had a normal busy week this September (2009), attending a three-day conference in Germany, coming home for two days to produce the two national tapes I do each month before heading off to Jacqueline's to attend the Liberal Party conference, and then straight up to London for a Ricability meeting. Ricability is an independent consumer research charity that tests products and services for the disabled and elderly and produces helpful and unbiased consumer reports. I am a trustee of this organisation.

In my initial telephone conversation with the NFB's Stan Bell he had asked me if I believed in integrated education, as this was one of the policies of the Federation. As I had been to an ordinary school, even though I had struggled to see the blackboard and small print in books, I was still pleased that I had not had to leave my family and friends to go to a special school. It was only six months after I had joined the Federation that I was nominated for its executive council. I can remember sitting at my first annual delegates' conference in Coventry, listening to the then president, Dr Fred Reid, and Charles Taylor, who must have been chairing Standing Orders as he was running the conference. I was quite amazed how efficiently the conference was conducted, and I never dreamed that 20 years later I would be in the president's chair.

When the election results were announced I could not believe how well I had done. I was only one vote away from being on the executive council. Only three months later, when one of the executive members resigned due to her mother's ill health, I was asked to take her place. As I was interested in access problems and there were other environmental issues to tackle in 1973, it was suggested by Colin Low, the Federation's general secretary, that we should establish an Environment Committee, for which I was elected as chairman, and I have continued in this post to the present day. Ironically, it is Colin, now Lord Low of Dalston, who has written the Foreword for this book.

One of the subjects we were to cover was access for guide dogs, and representation on the Guide Dog Council. Regrettably, the latter has still not been achieved. My first deputation was to the Guide Dog Council and, as a result, a liaison committee was set up in 1974. A meeting took place every quarter for ten years, where we discussed various issues with the chairman of the Guide Dog Council, the director of training and other representatives. It was during those years that I was responsible for campaigning for access for guide dogs. The Guide Dog Association did not think it was their job to campaign and so they left it up to the Federation. It took eight years of writing letters to British Rail and holding meetings with them before they changed their policy to allow guide dogs in dining carriages and sleeping cars. This turnaround only came about after I questioned Peter Parker, the British Rail boss, on the Jimmy Young show on BBC radio. This was one of the campaign issues that I was able to raise and get support for at the National Consumer Congress, which I attended for 17 years as a Federation representative.

It was at a National Consumer Congress event, held at Liverpool University, that I was able to put into practice a fire escape procedure that I had been taught at Leamington Spa Guide Dog Training Centre. It was 3 o'clock in the morning when I heard the fire alarms go off. I got out of bed, put on my coat and shoes, attached Topsy's lead and harness and exited my room. Other delegates called out, "Are you alright, Jill?" I said, "Yes, but we had better get out." Apparently all the lights had gone out, so I had to lead the sighted delegates along the corridor and down three flights of stairs to the safe area.

The Council for the Disabled had a special sign for access, but they would not add a guide dog to it, so I suggested creating a sign that said, "No dogs allowed except guide dogs". These signs were produced and displayed in food shops and restaurants so that people knew that guide dogs would be allowed in. It took 11 years to change the policies of Butlin's and Pontin's holiday camps, and even longer in the case of the House of Commons.

When you are campaigning you need to hear everybody's point of view, and so I naturally wanted to be able to sit in the public gallery of the Commons to listen to relevant debates. It all came to a head in 1984 when I wanted to go and listen to the cycle tracks debate but access was denied. I had been campaigning for about nine years to be allowed access to the gallery and at the same time had been campaigning about the dangers of cycling on pavements and the need for dedicated cycle paths with separate pedestrian walkways, so it was very important that I listened to that debate. It annoyed me to think that anyone else could go in and listen to that debate, even if it held no particular interest for them, and yet I could not. This issue created a lot of publicity and one phone call I received was from a blind man called David Blunkett. He said that he supported what I was doing, as one day he hoped to become a Member of Parliament and would require access for his guide dog. I suggested that he joined the Federation to help us with our campaigning, but he declined. The House of Commons policy was eventually changed in 1987, and subsequently David Blunkett got his wish too.

When we formed the Environment Committee for the NFB in 1973, my experience on the Southend Access Committee stood me in good stead for the work I would be doing in the future. Although the Environment Committee's job was to implement the resolutions passed at the annual delegates' conference, it was also necessary to take part in national conferences held by government and national organisations.

It was not long before I was attending regular meetings with the Department of Transport in Marsham Street in London. With Topsy as my guide, we would make the half-hour walk to Chalkwell station. There was no bus service back then or even today. We would then take the train to Barking, catch the underground train for the 45-minute journey to Westminster station, and then walk round Parliament Square to Marsham Street.

One of our first conferences at the Department of Transport was a meeting with many other disability groups. I found out that there was a group called the Joint Committee on Mobility for the Disabled (JCMD) and asked if there were blind people on that committee. I can remember the answer very well: blind people do not have mobility problems, so they would not have a blind person on their committee. Well, that answered a lot of questions. At that time there was an orange 'disabled' parking badge to which blind people were not entitled, as well as a financial benefit, and kerbs were being lowered, making the pavement and road division extremely dangerous for blind people. I wrote letters for eight years to the JCMD, but they simply would not have anyone with a sensory disability on their committee.

Eventually we formed the Joint Committee on Mobility for the Blind and Partially Sighted. This was a coordinating body for all the national organisations that were concerned with mobility and transport issues for blind and partially sighted people as well as deaf/blind people. After the first chairman died a couple of years later, I became the chairperson and remained in that role for eight years.

After a lot of campaigning by the Federation and Lord Alf Morris, the orange badge was extended to cover blind people. Nowadays it is a blue badge, which can be used throughout Europe. We held many public demonstrations during the eighties and, as a result, in 1991 the Disability Living Allowance (DLA) and the Attendance Allowance were introduced, which included blind and partially sighted people.

I was thrilled to bits to be appointed as a member of the Disability Living Allowance board by Sir Nicholas Scott, then Secretary of State for Social Security, and I served on that board for seven years. At the same time I was appointed to sit on Appeals Tribunal Service panel, a role I still perform today about twice a month, although it now comes under the Ministry of Justice. The panel comprises myself, as someone with extensive experience of a wide range of disability issues, together with a judge, who is a legal representative, and a medical doctor. We are an independent tribunal that, based on the evidence we have received and read (all the papers are read to me prior to the tribunal date) and a subsequent meeting with the appellant, assesses whether a person meets the criteria laid down in the benefits regulations. I really enjoy the work, but after hearing the life that some people have to cope with due to their disabilities it makes me feel very humble and lucky.

When the DLA benefit was introduced in 1991 there were two components, one relating to care needs and the other based on mobility. There are three levels for care - low rate, middle rate and higher rate. Blind and partially sighted people can apply for all three levels and will be assessed according to their needs to determine which level should be awarded. The mobility allowance is a different kettle of fish and goes back to that original statement by the JCMD.

The mobility component comprises two levels - lower rate and higher rate, and when the benefit was first introduced blind people were only entitled to the lower rate. While on the DLA board, and subsequently as a Federation representative on the RNIB's Disability Allowance Coordinating Committee, I had always argued that blind people should be entitled to the higher rate of the benefit. Although we can walk, we cannot see where we are walking, we cannot drive cars or ride bikes and, therefore, we do have a mobility problem. It took years to persuade the RNIB to campaign on this issue, but eventually they did and after a couple of mass lobbies by blind people we were awarded the higher mobility rate in March 2009, but we will not actually be able to apply for the benefit until 2011.

At the Department of Transport, our small group of disabled people, led by Ann Frye and Sir Peter Baldwin, started to get a lot bigger, and we were becoming involved with a lot of work trying to improve the transport needs for a wide range of people with disabilities, but in the knowledge that any access improvements would help everybody.

In 1985 our committee became part of the Transport Act and a Statute Committee and became known as the Department of Transport Advisory Committee for Disabled People. Linda

Chalker was the minister at the time, and she did so much to help the committee's work.

One of the first topics we covered was buses. My mum was waiting for a hip replacement and was having problems getting up the high step onto the bus, and as I am short - four feet eleven inches to be precise, I had always struggled to reach the bell push on the ceiling. Even when I could see with one eye my vision was not good enough to read the number of the bus, and I had to rely on the conductor calling out the name of the stop. I also tried to make good use of any colour contrasts on the bus, but these were few.

So, with all these ideas, we formed a group to draw up a standard for bus design. This included a low floor entrance, a reachable bell push, colour contrasting on all the handrails and good lighting. We also produced a video for staff training. While this was going on at national level, the branches of the Federation were campaigning at local level to lobby the bus companies and help to train bus staff. Although work has been done to improve bus design, there is still no requirement to have audible announcements. These are very much needed for blind people, so that they know where they are on their journey and when they have arrived at their destination.

Eventually, an electronic talking bus stop was trialled in Weston-super-Mare. We all travelled down to Weston by coach, to launch what was known as ELSIE (Electronic Signalling and Indicating Equipment). This meant that you could stand at a bus stop and be told how long the next bus would be and its number. Through lack of money this pilot was not continued, and it is only now, in late 2009, that a similar project is being put into operation, so I was amazed when I went to Prague in 1997, as chairperson of the EBU Commission on Mobility and Guide Dogs, to discover that this system was in place on every bus, tram and train. I have been to Prague four times over the past 12 years and have used it. Why it takes our country so long to develop such simple but helpful systems I shall never know.

Likewise, with the Black Cab taxi, we got the colour-contrasted handles installed quite quickly, but to date they still do not have a talking meter.

After years of fighting we eventually got the Disability Discrimination Act passed, and in accordance with that Act all taxis are supposed to allow the transportation of guide dogs. However, I have experienced difficulty on many occasions when trying to get a taxi and it can mean a long wait before one will pick me up with my dog. Drivers who do not want to have a dog on board will simply refuse to stop for me, or they will not respond to the call if I try to book a taxi from home. This reluctance can be due to religious grounds, where drivers are from ethnic backgrounds. I always say that my guide dog is much better behaved than I am, and that she will just curl up and go to sleep on the floor.

The Federation had campaigned ever since 1957, when the first audible signal was installed on a pedestrian crossing, and over the years different kinds of audible signals have been introduced. First came the Pelican (Pedestrian Light Controlled, more commonly known as Pelican) crossing, then the Puffin (Pedestrian User-Friendly Intelligent) crossing and finally the Toucan crossing (meaning two can cross together, the pedestrian and the cyclist).

Southend was the experimental town chosen to have audible signals installed on ordinary sets of traffic lights. This means that when all the traffic lights change to the red phase an audible sound indicates that it is safe to cross the road. In fact this system operates on some traffic lights close to where I live, right outside Alvin's music shop.

As many deaf and hard of hearing people could not hear the audible signal, a cone-shaped rotating knob was installed, enabling those with hearing disabilities to use their sense of touch. This is located under the button panel and turns when it is safe to cross. This kind of rotating cone should only be installed in addition to the audible signal and not instead of it, as many people with hand disabilities cannot feel the cone and others may have a guide dog in one hand and a shopping bag or trolley in the other, so they do not have a hand free to feel for the cone.

Also we are trained, with a long cane or guide dog, to go to the centre of the panel to cross, but to press and feel the button you must move to the pedestrian post, which can be many feet away.

By the time you get back to the middle of the crossing sometimes you have missed the safe time to cross and, as that time is limited, you should only cross at the start of the audible signal.

Zebra crossings can be dangerous, as a car approaching from one direction might stop to let you cross, but one coming in the other direction might not. Also another car might try to overtake the car that has stopped and cross in front of you. Although not actually at a crossing, that happened to me outside my church, three minutes' walk from my house, and the overtaking car nearly knocked me down. Some drivers will hoot their horns, but I never respond to that as there is no certainty that it is meant as a signal for me. If you really want to help someone, then stop your car and offer assistance. Let the blind person take your arm and then escort them right across the road. As mentioned earlier, the development of new hybrid silent cars will add to these dangers and blind people will need more help in the future.

CHAPTER 11 – DISABILITY DISCRIMINATION AND DESIGN FOR ALL

It was on one of my weekly walks with my guide dog Topsy that I thought of a solution to the problem that I and other blind people were having with the flattening of kerbs for wheelchairs.

Without thinking, I had been using a change of surface to identify where I was in a street and when I was approaching a gate. Every Thursday I used to visit a friend called Peg Gargan in Highfield Grove, which was at the other end of Westcliff to where I lived. It took Topsy and me about half an hour to walk there, crossing many roads, and when I turned into Peg's road I walked until I felt this change of surface under my feet, and then I would say to Topsy, "Find Peg's gate," which was just a couple of feet away.

This was at the time that we had established our little group of people at the Department of Transport to talk about the transport needs of disabled people and I had pointed out that the dropping of kerbs was a hazard for blind people. So Sir Peter Baldwin, who was Under-Secretary of State at the Department, brought together two groups of people: those representing the blind people, and a group of wheelchair users. The blind argued that the kerb needed to be at least four inches high so that they knew where the pavement ended and the road started, and the wheelchair users said that they must have a totally flat kerb. In the middle sat me with my idea of a textured pavement like the one in Highfield Grove. That was a bit like a slab of chocolate, a flat cobbled effect. It was completely flush to the road, so any pram or wheelchair would have found it very easy to negotiate. Everyone present agreed that we must find a solution for safety reasons.

The next step was that two gentlemen - I can remember that one was called Neil Duncan, from the Transport Road Research

Laboratory (TRRL) - came to spend a day with me. I showed them the tactile pavement and took them for a walk around to explain what was needed. We walked along Southend seafront and I pointed out that even though there were pedestrian crossings there was no way for me to know where they were.

So, after two years' research, a group of about 20 people, with various disabilities, went to the TRRL at Crowthorne to test out different kinds of textures. We were taken round individually and at the end we all agreed on the 'Blister' pattern that was eventually chosen. This texture was a little more pronounced than I had wanted, but it had to be like that for blind people who are diabetic, as a side effect of diabetes is a loss of feeling in the feet. I have explained to anyone that has complained about the texture the reasoning behind its introduction - to stop blind people from walking onto a road without realising and risking being hit by a car and possibly killed, particularly those with diabetes, and at the same time to enable people in wheelchairs to cross the road safely and easily - and they quickly understand.

It was on 18th July 1983 that Tony Newton, then Secretary of State for Social Security, launched the textured pavement in Parliament Square. It was only the previous November that I had suggested that the first one should be laid outside the Commons, so that all the Members of Parliament would be fully aware of the facts when their constituents asked them to have it installed in their own areas.

It was Tony Newton who appointed me as a member of the newly formed Access Committee for England in March 1984. Through that committee's work, and as chairperson of the Joint Committee on Mobility for the Blind and Partially Sighted, we introduced other kinds of textures to indicate steps and the edges of railway platforms.

Unfortunately, many local authorities have laid the textured paving incorrectly and it certainly does not give the safety information to blind people that was originally intended.

Over the past 26 years blind people have relied on the tactile paving to indicate where there is a safe place to cross the road, by feeling with their feet, and it is coloured red so that people with partial sight can see it. It has been introduced in other parts of the world too, but as yet there is no International Standard.

It is quite clear from recent developments that planners and local authorities do not understand how difficult and dangerous negotiating the environment can be for those that are totally blind or deaf/blind. Since I took over the EBU Commission on Mobility and Guide Dogs in 1997 it has become even more apparent that many towns and cities in Europe have been designed without any consideration of the needs of people with disabilities.

About five years ago we were made aware of a new concept for our streets. This not-so-bright idea, which came from the Netherlands, was to have shared facilities for cyclists and pedestrians. The scheme would involve removing all the pavements and all the pedestrian crossings and making the street one level. Drivers of all vehicles would have to make eye contact with the pedestrian and it would be a case of each one fighting for their space. These shared streets are now being introduced all over the country and, despite all the representative organisations for the blind protesting and lobbying against them, they are still being introduced.

I was really pleased to be invited to speak at the European Road Safety Day conference in Paris in 2008. It was attended by 600 delegates from all parts of Europe, and I had to speak about the vulnerable road user. It was very clear to me that millions of pounds had been spent on these shared streets, and yet no thought had been given to the needs of blind people. Blind people must have a pavement to walk on safely and do need a pedestrian crossing to negotiate busy roads, otherwise they are risking their lives. I was speaking from personal experience, as it was just one week after I had nearly been killed in Rome, having found myself in a shared street. The only way I know that I am as safe as I can be is when I am on a pavement. It is bad enough having to cope with overhanging branches, lamp posts, bollards, rubbish sacks, cars, bikes and all the other obstacles that have to be negotiated, but at least I feel safe. I certainly would not feel safe without a pavement. Also, children are taught to stop, look and listen before they step off the kerb. What will they do in a shared street?

We were fortunate that the Department of Transport in the

seventies and eighties recognised the dangers of flattening kerbs and supported the introduction of tactile pavements, but sadly the current administration does not appear to do so. It is a frightening thought that the increasing number of elderly and disabled people over the coming years may not have safe pavements and safe pedestrian crossings to walk on. In cases where members of the Federation have been able to talk to their local councils and explain the dangers of this new concept, the proposed schemes have been stopped.

Another new hazard for blind people, as mentioned earlier, is the hybrid electric vehicle. While these are good for cutting pollution, they are very quiet and hearing them coming would prove difficult. Bikes can be hard to hear too, but at least when I have been struck by a cyclist on the pavement I have not suffered any injury; a silent car would be a different matter and the outcome could be fatal.

I wonder why it is that these fit and able-bodied planners, architects and engineers never consider the needs of those of us that are not blessed with the same? It is only when someone in one's own family is affected with a disability that we start to understand.

Following that conference in Rome I attended the annual International Day for Disabled People in Brussels. The theme for that conference was 'Designing for All'. Unfortunately, most of the people attending that conference were disabled and, although these conferences are good in some ways, I think conferences where you can influence governments, councils and the general public are much better.

Twice a year I attend a railways meeting in Brussels, as a representative of the EBU, and I travel there on Eurostar. This is such an easy journey for me now, as there is a station at Ebbsfleet in Kent. It only takes 45 minutes by car to the station and then just under two hours on the train. As yet, I cannot travel back into Ebbsfleet with my guide dog, as they do not have facilities for checking dogs coming into this country. I go just for the day and instead of Amanda I take a sighted friend, usually now Pam Martin, who is also my regular taxi driver. Pam also takes me to airports when I have to go on my many other trips abroad.

Although I enjoy the trips it is very hard work, involving a lot of concentration, and is very tiring. One compensation is the lovely food and red wine, as well as the good company of friends and colleagues. Sometimes we stay in hotels and at other times in very nice centres that have been specially built for blind people. Denmark, Finland, Sweden and Norway have such centres.

My daughter Jacqueline has only travelled abroad with me twice for meetings, mainly because she had young children to look after but lately because she works. She came to Norway with me and also to Paris, when I was organising a transport conference. Normally Peter and I will have just one sighted escort between us, but on that occasion we needed two helpers as it was a large conference.

I have attended many meetings and conferences in Brussels in the parliament building, where I have met and appeared on television with my European Member of Parliament, Richard Howitt.

My experiences of travelling abroad helped to highlight various issues that needed to be addressed. The first resolution passed by the EBU Assembly was the need for a Europe-wide concessionary travel card. Most countries have their own travel card but they cannot be used in other countries. Despite many letters and meetings on this subject, we still have not achieved our objective.

One objective that has had a successful outcome, however, is the introduction of new air regulations, which were put in place in July 2008. Prior to this, the responsibility for providing disability assistants lay with individual airlines, but now airports are required to give disability awareness training so that assistance can be given to anyone with reduced mobility.

In the past, blind people were automatically put in a wheelchair rather than being offered a guide to accompany them to and from the plane. Those that have physical disabilities or who are elderly may well need a wheelchair, but it should be offered rather than being insisted upon. Even when travelling with my guide dog, I have still been asked if I need a wheelchair.

For the past six years I have been able to travel abroad with my guide dog, but it has proved very expensive. I have to pay for the rabies vaccination and booster prior to travelling overseas, and I also have to pay the vet in Majorca about £40 for the treatment required before I can return to the UK with my guide dog.

One of the issues that still concerns me is the design of white goods. Over the years, as technology has advanced, very little notice has been taken of the needs of blind people. For example, it is very difficult to find a washing machine, a dishwasher or a toaster that does not have a visual display panel, and when buying a cooker you have to choose one that can have a Braille panel installed. However, a lot of blind people do not learn Braille and many are elderly, and it is very difficult for them to cope with such machines. For me it is particularly frustrating trying to find white goods with good colour contrasts and clear print for Alvin to see, as well as ones that can be operated by touch. In addition, the instruction books are never available in large print, Braille or on tape when you buy these items. You always have to wait, sometimes for months, for aids to be provided; in one case I waited a whole year for a Braille cooker panel. No sighted person would put up with such a service, so why should blind people have to do so? We pay the same price for our goods and yet we get second-class service.

I can remember a meeting that Colin Low and I had with William Hague, who was then Minister for the Disabled. I had just qualified with my fifth guide dog, Lady. One of my concerns was that, although the Disability Discrimination Act had been passed, it did not cover transport or education, and did not address the white goods problem. White goods in the UK are usually designed and built overseas, so we have to wait for international legislation to be passed.

It was as a member of the RNIB's Consumer Committee that I attended a meeting with the Bank of England, to help design the new bank notes. This was very difficult, as for those six years we had to keep the discussions confidential. The Bank of England had wanted to make all their notes the same size, which would have made it impossible for blind people to tell one from another. As I was sworn to secrecy, I could not even report back to the

Federation. After six years of meetings and standing firm, the new notes were introduced, each one a different size. The Consumer Committee, which unfortunately no longer exists, also used to test out any new items that the RNIB planned to sell.

I have spent over 30 years sitting on RNIB committees. Initially I was elected by the members of the Federation to act as their representative, and subsequently I was elected by the RNIB membership to sit on the new Assembly for six years, when it transformed from a Council. For many years I was a governor for various RNIB schools and colleges, and also chaired Group D, which coordinated the blind people's organisations that sat on the RNIB Council as well as various sub-committees of the RNIB, covering a wide range of subjects, and I have sat on the international committee since 1988.

Over the past few years there has been a lot of talk about recycling. In an attempt to implement their duty under the Disability Discrimination Act, Southend Council asked whether I or the members of the local branch of the Federation could find out if refuse collections were causing any problems for the blind or disabled. At that time we had two sacks, one black and one pink. The black one was for general rubbish and the pink one was for paper.

Well, in my office at home, I have a large plastic bin the size of a dustbin. As you can imagine, I have a lot of waste paper. If it got full and Alvin was not around, I would go and get a new bag from the kitchen. As the pink and black sacks were the same size and shape, I would often replace the full sack with one of the wrong colour.

As a result, I wrote a letter to the Council contractor, Corries, suggesting that we should have sacks of different textures to enable differentiation between the two. It was only a few months later that three different sacks were designed, and now they are used by all the residents of Southend. The smooth black sack is for general rubbish, the pink textured one is for paper and glass, and the white one with distinctive handles is for textiles. We now also have a square box for recycling food.

Many councils provide wheelie bins, which are a hazard in themselves. Again, they are of different colours, but most give no indication of the colour for blind people. I did suggest that the Slade colour button code used for marking clothes could be used for the bins. This was a simple, low-cost but effective solution. Councils could do so much more to help blind people just by talking to us and listening to us.

So often it is the well-meaning sighted people that run clubs and societies who decide what services to give to blind people, without finding out what is really needed. This emphasises the importance of organisations such as the NFB, which is run solely by blind and partially signed people, except for one or two sighted members of staff in the Wakefield office, and all our members work in a voluntary capacity.

Even though some areas have a talking newspaper, the quality of these papers varies from town to town. Some will read just the news, whereas others will include deaths, births and marriages, and also other local information. Quite often reports cover an event that has recently taken place, but it would be so much more helpful to hear an advert for an upcoming event to give us the opportunity to attend.

I, like most blind people, have to wait until a friend or neighbour can spare the time to come and read post or other printed material. If a blind person lives alone, this might mean waiting for a couple of weeks to have their post read, which could lead to late payment of bills and missed appointments. It would be really helpful if there were some kind of locally run reader service that a blind person could contact to request a reader when they needed it.

My local shops have meant a lot to me, giving me the incentive to go out, even on days when I have felt depressed and the weather is bad. Our weekly visit to the local butcher, Mark, gives us the opportunity to have fresh meat each day, which is much healthier for us than having processed food from the supermarket. We do miss our local greengrocer, which had to close down a couple of years ago.

The other important local shop for me is the post office. Although the main Chalkwell post office was closed down a few years ago despite a very vigorous campaign to keep it open, supported by our local Member of Parliament, David Amess, we still have the one on Eastwood Boulevard. I depend on this facility to get my pension and my cash as well as any banking services I need, as we have no bank in the Chalkwell area.

It is wonderful to see all the progress that has been made over the years, even though securing changes has often involved a long fight, but there is so much more still to do and there are always new challenges on the horizon.

CHAPTER 12 – MOVING ON
IN MY PERSONAL LIFE

1977 was the Queen's Silver Jubilee year, and for our carnival float that year we built a two-tier cake. I must have made about 10,000 roses, and Mick built a model of the Queen's coach and horses out of polystyrene tiles. We won first prize in the Southend, Rochford and Burnham carnivals. Jacqueline was not even on our float, as her Girls' Brigade band was leading the procession.

It was while I was building the float that I popped round to the butcher's for some shopping, and another customer told me that Alvin would be coming home with his new guide dog that Friday. I was not sure whom she meant. The lady explained that I probably had met him before, as he used to own the shop next to Mick's workplace. I remembered that Mick had told me about a man who had a talking book even though he was not really blind. Apparently, he had now lost his sight almost completely and was training to be a piano tuner in London. I told her to tell Alvin to introduce himself to me if he saw me out, and that occasion came only a couple of days later outside the same shop. Topsy had stopped as she had seen Alvin's new dog, Unity. We had a little chat and I said that he and his wife should pop round to our house at some point but that at the moment I was busy with the carnival float. Strangely, that butcher's shop is now Alvin's own music shop, where he sells musical instruments and records.

Alvin did pop round, but after that I did not hear from him again until around November, when he phoned to say that he wanted to join the Federation. I soon found out that Alvin had married his wife Jane on the rebound from a broken relationship and apparently she had lied about her age when they met. Alvin was 29 at that time and Jane had told him she was 49, but he discovered after they were married that she was actually 59. They divorced ten years later.

At that time I was travelling every week to London for meetings at the RNIB and the Department of Transport. I had always travelled to Fenchurch Street station by train and then had taken a taxi. I started to travel with Alvin some days, and he taught me how to use the underground. Alvin still had a little vision and knew his way round the underground very well, as he had lived most of his life in the East End of London. He gave me a lot of confidence, and we gradually became good friends. I can remember having conversations on the train about blind people who were married to each other, never dreaming that ten years later we would marry each other.

It was not until 18th July 1983 that I made the most difficult decision of my whole life: to leave Mick and go and live with Alvin. It was not a decision I had taken lightly. I know that if I had not left I would have ended up having a nervous breakdown. I did try to go back to Mick three times, but it was never going to work. So finally, on 7th August, I left for good and Mick filed for divorce straight away. The situation was not helped by the local and national press, who were constantly on my doorstep or phoning me to find out what was going on. They could not understand why I, a blind woman, would leave a sighted husband to go and live with a blind man. I told them that it was a private matter and was nothing to do with them. They even took a photo of Alvin and me while we were taking the dogs for a walk, without our knowing.

It was only a few months later that Mick decided he did not want to live in our house anymore as he was getting married again. So Alvin bought Mick's share of the house and we both moved there in December 1984. Jacqueline lived with Alvin and me until she moved into her own flat with her boyfriend, Mike, in 1988.

Alvin and I did not get married until 1987, really because we were both too busy. As it happened, the day we chose, 10th January, turned out to be one of the worst days of the winter, with heavy snow, and many of the guests had to leave the reception early to travel back to their homes. We held our reception at the Esplanade pub on the seafront at Southend, which at the time was run by two friends, Betty and John Harper, who had been fellow students at Municipal College. Now they live in Majorca, and Betty comes with me on some of my trips abroad.

We decided to have our honeymoon in Majorca. Alvin had never been abroad before, so it was a totally new experience for him, and although the weather was not perfect it was certainly a lot better than it was in England. I had not been abroad since working in Guernsey in 1956 to the time that Mick and I split up. Jacqueline had taken me to Amsterdam for five days in 1985, and as we got on well we thought we would then go to Majorca. We went just for one week and stayed in the Grand Fiesta hotel in Playa de Palma, the same hotel that Alvin and I chose for our honeymoon. Jacqueline and I went on three coach trips all over the island, which gave me a wonderful picture of Majorca. We returned there the following year for another week, and also holidayed together in Tenerife and Lanzarote.

I was unable to take my guide dog abroad with me due to the quarantine regulations at that time, so for the first time in her life Jacqueline had to guide me and generally help me to find my way around in the hotels. It was at that time that I started another campaign to get the quarantine regulations changed. I met up with Lady Mary Fretwell, who started the Passports for Pets charity. Mary used to look after my guide dog, Lady, until the regulations were changed. My latest guide dog, Amanda, comes with us each time we go to Majorca. Amanda knows her way round Palma Nova just as well as she does Westcliff.

Alvin and I have been to Majorca every year for our annual holiday. It is cheaper to go abroad in the winter than stay in a hotel in this country. We have always been accompanied by a sighted friend, even on our honeymoon, when Barbara and John Armitage came with us. On the Sunday Barbara drove us to Palma Nova to find the English-speaking church, but we never did locate it, although we did find the beautiful bay of Palma Nova, where we have been every year since for our holidays. However, in 1989, John became Mayor of Southend, which meant that he and Barbara would not be able to spare the time to come on holiday with us.

I had heard on a radio travel programme that Thompson's, the holiday company, had a helpline that offered assistance to disabled people who wanted to travel abroad, so I decided to give them a call. I think the lady I spoke to was rather surprised when I told her that we were both blind and were thinking about going to Majorca on our own. I explained that we had been to the hotel in Palma Nova three times and knew the layout of the hotel, even the short walks to the small local shops, but that we would need some help getting from the airport to the coaches, and from the coach to the hotel. The Thompson's lady told me that she had two blind brothers and would not dream of letting them go abroad by themselves. When I asked her why, she said that they might fall down some steps and hurt themselves, but my response was that they could do that just as easily in this country. After a long discussion, the telephone conversation ended with her saying, "You must let me know if you decide to go."

Well, I did not let her know, and I went straight round to my travel agent and booked two weeks' holiday at the Santa Lucia Hotel in Palma Nova, Majorca. The attitude of that lady made me very cross, and so we were determined to make a success of our holiday. The staff at Gatwick and Palma airports gave us all the help we needed, and when the coach stopped outside the hotel there was a man at the door to meet us. His name was Stan and he said that he was from Help the Aged and offered to help us. We really thought that Thompson's had laid on this help after all, but no such luck. Stan was actually a holidaymaker who had just happened to be there as we arrived, and back home in Kent he worked for Help the Aged. He was on his own and was recovering from a heart attack. He had been there for two weeks and did not know what he was going to do with his third week, so he spent that week coming out for walks with us, which gave us so much confidence, so much so that when he went home we were able to go out on our own. We spent most of the daytime swimming in the outside pool and the evenings dancing. Other guests were amazed that we could dance so well when we were blind. Alvin had just enough vision to guide me round the floor without knocking too many people over.

When in Majorca we spend nearly every evening in Munroe's Bar just across the road from the Carla Blanca hotel where we stay. Alvin likes to sing karaoke and we both like to dance to the music played by Andy. Because I passed all my medals for ballroom and Latin American dancing before I went blind, I find it quite easy to dance and just love it. I always preferred ballroom and Latin American dancing to the modern sequence dancing, which Alvin calls sheep dancing, as everyone follows everyone else. I do miss being able to watch dancing on the television, but at least I can dance, which is something a lot of other people with physical disabilities cannot do. I learnt modern sequence dancing when Mick and I went to Butlin's holiday camp back in 1969. In fact we won the beginners' cup at the end of the week, and when we returned home we joined a local club and continued with the dancing for five years, until the time that I decided to stand for the Council and was too busy with canvassing on top of my other commitments. And that was not the only prize awarded on that holiday. Jacqueline and I won the mother and daughter competition, wearing matching dresses that I had made and sporting exactly the same hairstyles. Jacqueline also won first prize in the fancy dress competition for her Jack in the Box outfit.

It is quite funny when Alvin and I stay at the hotel, as sometimes we go dancing in the hotel's ballroom until about ten o'clock and then leave to go across to Munroe's, and the rest of the guests say goodnight to us, thinking that we are going off to bed. Mind you, I think my guide dog thinks the same thing. But no early nights for us - and that includes the dog. My current guide dog, Amanda, is very good and goes to sleep under the table while Alvin and I get up to dance. In fact, she usually gets offered a drink before us! My fourth guide dog, Quella, always got up when 'Twist and Shout' was played and she would come out onto the dance floor and have a dance with me.

It is always interesting to hear people's reactions to Alvin and me when on holiday, when we are just doing the normal things that all the other holidaymakers enjoy. Because we are blind people make various comments, sometimes to our faces but more often about us in the background, as though we cannot hear what they are saying. I usually do my knitting while resting between dances or while sitting by the side of the swimming pool, and people are quite amazed that I can knit.

Alvin was a good swimmer and one day he was about to dive into the deep end of the pool when a well-meaning old lady went up to him, grabbed his swimming trunks, and pointed out, "That is the deep end," to which Alvin replied, "Yes, I know. I wouldn't be diving into the shallow end, would I?"

The general public could be a lot more helpful by giving us information, such as letting us know where there is a spare table with seats or offering help when we are waiting to cross a busy road and there is no pedestrian crossing. If you see someone with a guide dog or a white stick, always approach them on the opposite side to their mobility aid and offer assistance. If they say yes, let them take your arm and escort them across the whole road. I knew a blind man once who got knocked down and whose dog was injured when his sighted helper left him in the middle of the road.

The following year Stan booked to come on holiday with us and we had a lovely time together. Sadly, Stan died a year later, but we were so grateful for the help he had given us.

In addition to our holidays abroad, Alvin and I have enjoyed some wonderful ones in the UK. It was in 1985 that a couple of friends from the Federation, Lesley and David Kelly, said that they were going to Clacton for a week's holiday. Alvin and I thought it might be nice to go there as well and meet them on the beach where their friends had a chalet, so we booked bed and breakfast accommodation in Clacton.

Prior to our holiday, we had heard an advert on Essex radio for caravans at Point Clear, where Alvin had a caravan in the sixties, and when we arrived at Clacton and turned on our little portable radio, the first thing we heard was this same advert for the caravans.

It was the May bank holiday Monday and we were out for an early morning walk when we came across a telephone box. I have always had a good memory and could remember the phone number for enquiries about the caravans at Point Clear, so we decided to give them a call. We spoke to a man called Brian Tree, who said that we could go and have a look at the park there and then, so we found a bus and made the 20-minute journey down to Point Clear. Brian offered us a free weekend in a caravan so that we could see how we liked it.

We returned on 21st June, accompanied by my daughter Jacqueline. When we had visited in May it had been a boiling hot day, but the weekend in June was very wet. However, we loved the caravan and all the entertainment on site, and if we liked it when it was wet then we would certainly like it when it was hot, so we bought our first caravan that weekend. On the campsite there was a Chinese takeaway, and we were amused to find a notice on the door saying, 'Guide dogs only'. We presumed that we could go in as well!

Point Clear is 55 miles from our house in Westcliff, but that is where I can still go to relax. We kept caravans until 1997, at which point the high ground rent and the fact that Alvin simply could not get away from work enough meant that it was no longer worthwhile. I did not feel safe in the caravan on my own. However, around the sea wall, which circles the caravan park, there are houses and bungalows, and we thought it would be nice to buy one of these. At that time Alvin had sold his previous house, and so, in November 1997, we bought our little bungalow, which is situated right on the sea wall. I call it my rest home. It is so quiet, the air is so fresh and it faces south-west, so we have the sun at the front all day, and our visitors all comment on the fantastic view. About two minutes' walk away there is a very nice pub, where Alvin and I like to go for a dance - when I can drag him away from his music shop.

When we first visited Point Clear we could get a coach direct from home to St Osyth, but after a couple of years that stopped, so we now have to go by train or taxi or with kind friends who give us a lift. While travelling to Point Clear by train we made friends with a couple who had their own taxi business, Jon and Loraine. Sadly, Jon died suddenly of cancer a few years ago. Although Loraine has given up her taxi business, she still picks me up from the station when she can.

In July 2008 I was telling Loraine about my grandson Joseph, who had just come back from a school trip to Italy, and she said she had always wanted to go on a cruise there one day. As it happened, I too had always wanted to go on a cruise, but Alvin did not fancy the idea. So, in September 2008, Loraine and I went off on our first cruise around the Mediterranean, which I loved.

CHAPTER 13 – FAMILY LOSSES

Jacqueline was only one year old when my dad had his first thrombosis. He was very ill in hospital and nearly died. Although he got better, he was not well enough to return to work. He had worked in London for 43 years, except for his six years away in the Army, most of which was spent in Germany. He travelled daily on the train from Benfleet station to Fenchurch Street station, and then made the short walk to the Co-operative Wholesale Society building in Lennan Street, where he sold shoes.

My dad was a very kind and sensitive person. He used to get very upset because of my blindness and could not do enough to help me. He was very poor and lived from week to week, but would always find enough money to buy presents for my birthday and Christmas that he knew would help me. He never believed in hire purchase, but he knew how much I wanted a record player for my sixteenth birthday, so he broke his principles and bought me one on HP. I was thrilled to bits with it and only found out about the HP when I was still using it in my thirties, I let him know how much that had meant to me, as I just loved playing my records, even though I sometimes drove my parents mad with my music blaring out at all times of the day!

I remember buying my first long-playing record in 1957, while working at Shell in Houndsditch. There was a small record shop just off of Aldgate and the record was of Buddy Holly, who has remained one of my favourites.

He would love to come and take Jacqueline for walks in Chalkwell Park and take her on the swings and show her the animals, and would then like to come home and eat the hot cakes that I had made. I can remember that, during those years that I was involved in making carnival floats, he would come and sit for hours watching me sew the crêpe paper flowers, and he could not understand how I could do what I did without seeing.

It was in the busy year of 1978 when my dad had a stroke and spent three months in hospital, until he died on 27th June at the age of 69. I visited him every day while he was in Southend hospital, walking there with Topsy, and I never had any problem gaining access to the hospital with my guide dog. Even when my dad was in intensive care, the hospital phoned me to let me know that I could still visit with Topsy and that someone would look after her just outside the door. On the day of his funeral, Jacqueline, who was 14, was in Denmark with the Girls' Brigade band, playing in the Danish Musical Festival, so she did not have to make a decision whether or not to go to the funeral. The service was held at Benfleet Methodist Church, where my dad had been a Scout master and a steward of the church ever since he moved to Benfleet in 1937.

As I mentioned earlier, my dad loved his gardening. He had bought me a rose bush as an Easter present the year he died, and it continues to bloom in my front garden. His last birthday present to me was a cuckoo clock with raised hands, and I positioned this in my hall between the kitchen and dining-room doors, as the sound was a good directional aid. I was very sad that my dad had died so young. He had never smoked or drunk alcohol, as he was a very strict Methodist, but he did worry a lot and had suffered a lot of stress due to my mother's reaction to me and my blindness.

It was 12 years later, in January 1990, that one of the most difficult periods of my life began - the last three years of my mum's life. Alvin and I were on holiday at the time, and mum had a really bad case of the flu and was confined to bed. The doctor had visited her at home, but there was an ambulance strike at that time and they would not take patients to hospital unless it was life-threatening. Jacqueline and Mike visited mum the following week and she was really ill and complaining of a very stiff left leg. A Green Goddess ambulance took her to hospital, but it was too late, and on 26th February, my mum's 75th birthday, she had her left leg amputated. While she was having her operation I was at County Hall, Chelmsford, lobbying about the cuts to the home help service, not knowing that three years later my mum would have her home help cut, which was one of the reasons she gave up her fight for life.

I encouraged my mum to keep going so that she would be able to return to her active life and attend Jacqueline and Mike's wedding in June. I wonder now if I did the right thing, as her quality of life for those three years was very poor. My mum was in constant pain and suffered many hours of depression. She stayed in hospital for several weeks and was then transferred to Balmoral Rehabilitation Unit. It was while she was there that Jacqueline and Mike got married. She was able to travel to the church and spend a little time at the reception, although wheelchair-bound.

Mum eventually went back to her own bungalow at Benfleet. Although I had been promised by the hospital that someone would be there to meet us and help her to settle in, no one came that day. Social Services never did install a ramp or shower, and we really had to fight to keep her home help going. Because they could not give her any help at weekends or on bank holidays, every Friday night we had to get a taxi to bring her to our home so that Alvin and I could look after her. The taxi cost £25 for the eight-mile journey, with an additional £1 for her wheelchair. I asked Southend Social Services for some help myself, but they said that they could not help me because my mum lived in the Castle Point district and I lived in Southend. It did not seem to matter that Alvin and I were both blind. Alvin at that time had very little sight and had not yet had the corneal grafts that eventually restored some of his vision. So it was very difficult to cope with my mum over those three years.

One of the reasons that I encouraged my mum to persevere was so that she could go back to her job as secretary of the Westcliff branch of the Townswomen's Guild. Unfortunately, while she was in hospital the Guild changed their venue to the church hall, meaning that a flight of stairs would need to be negotiated. Although she struggled up them a few times it caused her so much pain that she eventually stopped going.

She could not visit many of her friends, as they did not have toilets on the ground floor. Fortunately, we'd had an extension built on our house in 1988 to accommodate a larger kitchen and also a dog run, as at that time we had three dogs. A toilet, shower and washbasin had also been added onto our dining room, which was all on one level. So all we had to do was buy a sofa bed and also a commode (as it was impossible for mum to get to the toilet during the night without her artificial leg) to turn it into a suitable place for mum to stay.

It was quite difficult to cope with my mum, as she got very depressed about what had happened to her and I know she had to suffer a lot. It was very hard for me not to say anything about my own blindness, which she had caused originally, but I had made that promise to my Auntie Rose and I would not break it.

I really had to battle with Castle Point Social Services to get mum the home help that I knew she needed. When I thought of the hours of voluntary service that my mum had given as an officer in the Girls' Life Brigade, it seemed disgraceful that we had to fight for this help.

It was on one Friday in July 1992 that my mum arrived with three letters. The first was from Social Services, saying that they were cutting her home help service to two days a week and for just one hour a day. The second was from Castle Point Council, notifying her that they were increasing her council tax. The last letter was from the Social Security department, telling her that they were stopping her income support. My mum had no money in the bank and no savings. She handed me those letters and said, "What is the point of living?" I could not answer her, and I walked out into the kitchen to have a secret cry.

It was only the following week that mum's home help noticed that her other foot had turned blue. She was admitted to hospital and never came out again. During those four months I visited her every day, usually accompanied by my friend, Arne, and after weeks of suffering she died on 19th October. In the August before she died she just understood that Jacqueline was pregnant and that I was going to become President of the NFB. I was at a Government reception at Conservative Central Office when the Prime Minister, John Major, whom I had met a few times before, asked me how I was. I told him about my mum, who had given up on life. I said, "Don't talk to me about the Community Care Act after the way my mum was treated and what she had to suffer." The Prime Minister just put his hand on my shoulder and said, "Don't!" He was choked and had to leave to go off to his weekly meeting with the Queen.

Ian Bruce, the Director-General of the RNIB, was with me at the time, and later he would often say to people, "You want to see Jill shock the Prime Minister!" John Major was a very nice man, and I think he was genuinely kind and understanding. I had first questioned him on the In Touch programme when he was the spokesman on disability, and I had asked him about cars parking on the pavements and why the Government had changed their policy.

Something I learnt to do when meeting a Minister was to shake their hand and keep hold of it until I had finished talking to them, as on previous occasions I had been left talking to myself, unaware that the other person had walked away. This has even happened at home. So please, when you have finished talking to a blind person, let them know that you are leaving.

Another problem I had in relation to my mum's death was that I did not know that she had taken out a policy with the All Church Life Insurance Company, which meant that on her death they were given her property, and my daughter and I did not receive one penny of my mum's estate.

At least I have got my memories, which no one can take away from me.

Over my lifetime, the attitude of people to me as a blind person has amazed me, shocked me, upset me and frustrated me, but it was taking my mother to church in her wheelchair that I will never forget, and my experiences stopped me from going to church for many years.

My mum and I had been members of Crowstone Church since 1955 and we had both served in the Girls' Brigade. So, when she was well enough to go out, all she wanted to do was to go to church. We decided to attend a service, so Alvin pushed mum's wheelchair on the half-hour walk to the church. At that time Alvin had very little vision, so it was very difficult for him. On arrival at the church we pushed the chair down the aisle and then helped mum into her pew seat. Alvin then pushed the chair round to a part of the church where it would be out of the way. No one offered to help. At the end of the service, everyone was invited for mince pies and coffee in the upstairs hall, which would have meant climbing two sets of stairs. The church did have a lower hall that could have been used and it had a level entrance. No one offered to get us a drink, so we just made our own way home feeling very depressed, and I have not been back to that church since. After all my mum had been through, I thought at least the Minister would have come to speak to us or visited us afterwards at home to apologise for the lack of understanding that the church had shown on that night - certainly not a Christian attitude.

Over the past few years I have attended Chalkwell Methodist Church, which is only a three-minute walk from my house. It was only on my second visit that they offered to get me a set of Braille hymn books, which arrived within two to three weeks. I do attend whenever I can, and I am always made to feel very welcome. I have rejoined the Ladies' Club, where I had been a member when I was first married. The church hall was where Jacqueline had gone to nursery school and where I had gone for my first walk alone. One of my happy memories was when they invited me to open their church fête.

Another member of my family who meant a lot to me was Uncle Bernard, my dad's youngest brother, and his death in 2000 has left a big hole in my life.

Since my dad passed away in 1978 Bernard had been like a father to me. Wherever I was in the world, either on holiday or at a meeting, I would always phone Bernard to tell him where I was. He looked after my grandma until she died at the age of 89, so that she did not have to go into a home for the elderly. He had sold the family home in Enfield years earlier and lived in a house on Canvey Island. He loved Canvey and never went away on a holiday, as he said he did not need to. Despite the fact that he had to take early retirement from the CWS because of spondylosis, he worked on a voluntary basis for 40 years for the Lifeboats (RNLI). They awarded him their gold medal, and when he received an MBE in 1998 I went with him, together with my cousin. I did not try to take my guide dog that time, as I knew they were still not allowed in.

The Southend crematorium was packed for Bernard's funeral, with many friends from Canvey and Enfield, including nurses who had looked after him for so long at home. Also at the ceremony was my friend Cynthia, who by this time was totally blind too. She used to meet Uncle Bernard in the local supermarket and he would tell her about any special offers. She also called him Uncle Bernard, and it was not until the time of Bernard's death that Cynthia's husband, Bob, realised that Bernard was not her real uncle.

I arranged for his ashes to be scattered on the sea at Canvey, where he had spent so much of the last years of his life and where, over many years, he had helped people to swim and saved people from drowning. The Southend lifeboat came in to Labworth beach with the lifeboat chaplain on board and Bernard's ashes. The coxswain, Colin, whom I knew from the days I went dancing at the studio when a teenager, came and stood behind me with a radio link to the boat, so that I could hear the chaplain speaking. That morning I had also collected some petals from the rose bush in my front garden that dad had bought me and they had gone with the ashes to the boat.

This was a very moving experience. The day had been wet and horrible but, just as the lifeboat came in, the clouds dispersed and the sun shone. One yellow petal lay on the water for a long while after most of the people had gone and the lifeboat flag had been lowered. It was as if my dad was saying goodbye to his younger brother.

CHAPTER 14 – BROADENING MY HORIZONS

September 1988 started a new chapter in my life. I, like any mother, was not looking forward to the day that Jacqueline would leave home, but as it turned out, although I was naturally upset, I was pleased as I knew she was very happy. She had been dating Mike for six years and they had saved hard to buy their own flat, which was only a 20-minute walk away. Mike's parents lived in the next road, and Mike and Jacqueline had first met at the bus stop while waiting for the bus to take them to college. I could not wish for a nicer son-in-law, and I have never had to worry too much about Jacqueline since she left home.

It was ironic that two weeks after Jacqueline left home I was set to attend my first conference abroad, held by the European Blind Union (EBU) for blind women. As the RNIB had no blind women on their international committee at that time, as a member of the RNIB Council I was invited to go. As I was unable to take my guide dog, I had to find someone to go with me, so my friend Barbara came as my escort.

The conference was held in Pordenoni, so I first travelled to Venice and it was quite exciting having to transfer from the plane to a taxi that was actually a boat. We stayed overnight in Venice and then travelled by train to Pordenoni. On arrival we were quite surprised to see dozens of men and no women, and we wondered if we had gone to the wrong hotel. But it turned out that at that time blind women in Italy were not allowed to take part in committee life. Only 14 women attended in total, one from each country. I spoke about being a blind housewife and mother, and it was decided that blind women must be allowed to take a more active part in the life of our communities, and especially within the EBU.

The following year the Women's Commission was formed, and I was elected to represent the UK and became vice-chairman. I served as a member of the Commission for six years and had the opportunity to travel to many parts of Europe. I also learnt an awful lot about the problems faced by blind women in the other member countries. I organised one of our meetings here in Southend, which was a great honour for me. It also brought back many memories, as it was the first time since my wedding day that I had returned to the Westcliff Hotel. Southend Council laid on a guided tour for our members, who had travelled from all parts of Europe. They took us down the Pier, to the sea-life centre, and then to Porters, the home of the Mayor.

Because of my interest in pavement and transport issues, I was always asking questions about the work of the Mobility and Guide Dog Commission. As a result, at the end of the three-year period, when the Commissions are reconstituted, I was taken off the Women's Commission and, much to my surprise, was elected as chairperson of the Mobility and Guide Dog Commission. Sir John Wall, president of the EBU and former chairman of the RNIB, had put my name forward for this post, and he telephoned me with this news from Eurostar while he was travelling home from the EBU board meeting. I really missed his help and advice after his sudden death in 2008. I took up the role in 1995 and I am still working on that Commission.

Although I had chaired many meetings in the UK, it was very different chairing my new Commission, as six out of the nine members could not speak English and each one had an interpreter to translate everything into their own language. This meant that I had to speak slowly and clearly and in short chunks, to give the interpreters time to translate. Listening to their constant chatter and concentrating on my own speaking has been quite a challenge. I never let a session go on for more than one-and-a-half hours, as it is very tiring for everyone. The Commission meetings cover all aspects of mobility, transport and guide dog work.

Our first meeting was held in Sicily and was organised by my vice-chairman, Giuseppe Castronovo. Even though he could not speak a word of English we got on very well, and at future meetings he always called me Madam President and bought me a large box of Italian sweets.

For the first few meetings I would do the minutes myself, and the RNIB helped with their circulation. But in 1996 I met Peter Wilkins at a Federation conference, and after he was made redundant as company secretary for BT he offered to become secretary for the Commission, a role that he continues to perform today. Peter, who has been blind from birth, attends the meetings and takes the minutes, and then he sends them out to all our members. Peter, born in Bolton in 1951, was a famous baby. His mother had quads naturally, and I can remember seeing a picture of them – three boys and a girl, all with black hair - on the front page of the Sunday Mirror. The quads were two months premature and, sadly, one boy died shortly after birth. Peter lost his sight as a result of receiving too much oxygen while he was being cared for in the baby unit. Peter now lives in Stockport, Cheshire.

I have been to Prague four times for meetings, and I have been so impressed with the development work they have done, especially Viktor Dudr, who invented a way-finding device that to date I think is the best in the world. Using a small transmitter about three inches long, a blind person can be told the number and destination of the bus, tram or train. It will also activate information at pedestrian crossings and at Prague airport.

I have learnt so much from travelling round the world and meeting so many blind and partially sighted people. After campaigning in this country since 1972, it was interesting to find out from my journeys overseas that the same hazards are present in every town and city throughout Europe. In fact, even in Australia we found cyclists and parked cars on pavements. This particular problem was the real reason why, in 1978, the NFB launched the 'Give Us Back Our Pavement' campaign. A member of the Federation, Ernie Patterson, produced a sticker to attach to cars that had parked illegally on pavements, thereby causing a hazard to blind pedestrians. I produced a series of leaflets that we could send out to anyone who might help us with the campaign. A friend designed a poster called 'Curb Pavement Hogs', which was paid for by the local Access credit card company. The campaign was aimed at the Department of Transport, the police and the general public, to make them aware of all the hazards on our pavements.

As I was public relations officer for the Federation at that time, I had to generate the publicity, and I was lucky enough to get the BBC journalist and newsreader Kate Adie to come for a walk with me round the block. This was featured on the nine o'clock news. I was also on the Jimmy Young show on Radio 2. We got a great deal of support for this campaign and a lot of publicity.

I was elected to be the first female president of the NFB in September 1992, at our annual delegate conference at Southampton. The NFB was formed in 1947, and although many other women had served on the Executive, none had served as president.

These were three very busy years. It started with my mum dying in the October, and in May 1993 my grandson Joseph was born, followed by my granddaughter Emily on the morning of our 1995 conference, which was held in Gateshead. Emily arrived about ten days early.

In June 1992 we launched the Get Streetwise video, which featured Tony Robinson and was funded by the Guide Dogs for the Blind Association. This video boosted the Give Us Back Our Pavement campaign, and we got a lot of national publicity for it. We achieved the highest Federation membership in its history, with 2,500 members.

In 1997 I was secretary for the Federation's golden jubilee conference in Solihul, and was conference secretary again in 2007, for the diamond jubilee held at the Albany Lions hotel, Eastbourne. This hotel had taken over from the town's RNIB's Palm Court hotel as the venue for an annual sixties weekend, which Alvin and I have organised every year since 2000. After the RNIB decided to close their specialist hotels for the blind, Mr Gulzar, owner of the Lions group of hotels, stepped in, and he has made us welcome ever since. Blind and partially sighted people and their friends travel from all parts of the UK to Eastbourne in January for this event. Alvin organises the karaoke and music, and his friend John Hills's sixties band plays live music for dancing in the hotel's large ballroom. Saturday and Sunday mornings are spent walking our guide dogs and shopping in the town, and in the afternoons we reminisce about the sixties: for some, their time at special schools for the blind;

and for me, struggling with my poor vision at a sighted school. After a cup of tea, Peter Wilkins hosts a quiz about the music, news and sport of the sixties, and we all have good fun. As this is an ordinary commercial hotel, I travel down the day before to give some awareness training, such as how best to serve food and drink to a large group of blind or partially sighted guests.

When I first made contact with Mr Gulzar he told me that the Council were complaining about the large life-size stone lions adorning the entrance to his hotel. I walked around the exterior wall of the Albany hotel and the lions were not overhanging or protruding, and they were actually very useful landmarks for any partially sighted people trying to locate the nearby Palm Court hotel. I then wrote to the Council to tell them that I thought it was a great pity that they were complaining about the lions, which were a useful and helpful landmark, and yet they were doing nothing about cars parked on pavements in the streets around the hotel or people cycling along the promenade, despite 'no cycling' notices. I was very pleased to learn that Mr Gulzar was allowed to keep his lions. In addition, he installed a lift with Braille and speech facilities and also a handrail leading up to the entrance doorway, although unfortunately there was no space for a ramp. Our weekends there are very enjoyable and no one can speak highly enough of the good service and excellent food.

Although the Southend Access Committee had operated for about ten years, it was quite clear that there was a need for a much larger organisation to fill the gaps in services and facilities for disabled people, and so the Southend Federation for the Handicapped was established. I was the chairperson for eight years and secretary for seven years, and for five of those fifteen years I organised Christmas shopping trips for the disabled. Since Southend high street had been pedestrianised in the 1970s it was apparent that many disabled people, including my own mother, had not been able to access the shops there, as they simply could not walk the distance from the bus stops.

I advertised in the Evening Echo, the local newspaper, for voluntary drivers and then had to link people, through the 40 organisations that had joined the Federation, with the drivers that came forward to help. Although this was hard work, I really enjoyed doing it.

Drivers of cars, minibuses and coaches would phone me, and I would Braille out the details, including name, address, size of vehicle, how many seats, if they could carry a wheelchair, etc. I would then draw up a separate list of disabled people, detailing their disability, what type of help they needed, and what kind of vehicle they could travel in. Some people came in groups from old people's homes, but the majority came from individual homes, and they usually numbered around 500 in total.

It was only on the week that the trip was to take place that I matched the two groups together. I also had to liaise with the shopkeepers to make arrangements for them to stay open for one evening, usually during the first week in December. This was to ensure that the shops were not too crowded and that each disabled person had someone there just to help them. I enlisted as many volunteers as I could to help with the scheme, including Scouts, Guides and Girls' Brigade members. We also had to take into account the weather. It did snow on a couple of occasions, but in those five years no one was let down. The disabled people really appreciated this help, and I even organised a shopping trip one July.

After my five-year involvement the Rotary Club offered to take over the scheme, but sadly it fizzled out and these special shopping evenings have not taken place for many years.

The Southend Federation also organised fêtes in Southchurch Park for many years, always on the first bank holiday Monday in May. These gave each organisation the opportunity to raise money for their individual charities, and it also gave local residents somewhere to visit over the bank holiday. A similar event was organised at Christmas, taking the form of a bazaar, and on one occasion it was opened by Timbo from BBC Essex. The Federation also organised exhibitions in Southend Library and the Civic Centre, inviting relevant companies to display aids and equipment that would be helpful to disabled people. The Federation eventually closed because no one was willing to become an officer. Everyone was too busy with their own organisations.

It was at one of these exhibitions that I met Rhona, who was working for the Electricity Board and was there to demonstrate various cookers that would be suitable for disabled people. Rhona became one of my regular helpers and she used to look after our guide dogs when we went abroad. She was one of the many friends that have taken Alvin or me supermarket shopping over the last 25 years.

When Rhona got married to her husband John I made their wedding cake, and when we took it to the reception venue at Hornchurch we were asked which catering firm had made the cake. On hearing that I had made it on my own, they just could not believe that a totally blind person could do anything like that.

I also made a wedding cake for one of the NFB members, who was getting married in Northumberland. This was rather a hair-raising occasion, as I was at a meeting in London and my husband had to bring the two cakes on the train and meet me at King's Cross to hand them over. The main line railway staff knew all about it, and I just had to have a lot of faith in them. The station I had to go to was not a scheduled stop, so the train company arranged for the train to make an additional stop so that I could get off with the cake. It was quite worrying on the journey when the guards changed and the new guard's announcements never mentioned any additional stops and said that the train would be going straight to Edinburgh. However, fortunately the guard eventually came to see me and told me not to worry and that they would be stopping for me.

The bridegroom, Mervyn Gee, was there to meet me, and so the journey was a success and the cakes were not damaged. Sadly, Mervyn and his new wife both died a couple of years later.

I am quite experienced not only at making cakes, but also at carrying them on trains, as I have had to do so on other occasions.

Since my daughter moved to Hampshire in 1997, I have taken Emily and Joseph's birthday cakes down there every year. It was not too bad when they were very young, but once their ages reached double figures this meant two cakes as my tins are in the shape of numbers. As Joseph likes fruit cake and Jacqueline, Mike and Emily like sponge cake I make one of each. On my visits Jacqueline usually takes me shopping in Southampton, so on my journeys down I have a trolley on wheels and a bag of cakes in one hand and my guide dog in the other! I really do have to depend on the help from railway staff.

I was thrilled to bits when I found out that the Jubilee line would be linking West Ham to Waterloo, but after trying it three times I went back to expensive taxis. There simply are not the staff to help at West Ham when transferring from the main C2C line to the underground.

One day, at Waterloo station, an accident taught me a lesson. My fifth guide dog, Lady, was nine years old, and we were getting on the train when she missed her jump onto the train and fell down onto the track. A member of staff was with me and quickly got help. They immediately stopped all the trains, saying, "Dog on track".

The driver came and took Lady's lead, which I was still holding, walked her to the end of the train and lifted her back up onto the platform. As she walked back to me, she was still wagging her tail, which was a good sign that she had not been hurt. The staff then got out the wheelchair ramps to ensure that we boarded the train safely, and this procedure was repeated at Southampton Central.

Following this incident I took Lady to the vet's for a check-up and found out that she had arthritis in her back legs. I wrote to South West trains and thanked them for all their help. I was very surprised to get a reply, thanking me for my thank you card and letter. It made me stop and think that, while having to write so many times about poor services, I should write a thank you letter or card each week. So from then on I started doing just that, and it is never too difficult to find someone who has helped me or my organisation. I think a little thank you goes a long way.

It was after I helped one of our Federation members, Alan, to get his DLA benefit that he sent me a bunch of flowers through the post as a thank you, and I was so thrilled with them. Until then I had not realised that you could order flowers through the post, and I have used that company ever since. Sadly, it was only three weeks later that Alan passed away.

Over the 36 years that I have chaired the Environment Committee of the NFB, I have made some very good friends, so, while we are talking about the importance of thanking people, I would like to pay tribute to some of those special people that are no longer with us.

Catherine Carter was the longest-serving secretary of the committee. She had a lovely personality and nothing was too much trouble for her. She worked full-time in the Labour Party head office, she was a guide dog owner and she was totally blind, with a hearing problem as well. She died a few years ago at a very young age. The Association of Visually Impaired Office Staff (AVIOS), on whose committee she also served, hold a Catherine Carter memorial event some years, on the theme of employment.

Another member and friend was Gordon Beale. He had been an active member of the Federation far longer than me, and when he died suddenly, just three days before his seventieth birthday, I was very upset. As I was the president at the time, at the end of my three-year term I presented a cup in Gordon's memory. He had been a true campaigner in Bradford, where he lived with his wife Louie. As Gordon had worked for the RNIB as well as sitting on many of their committees and we were both governors of the RNIB's Redhill College, I planted a tree in their grounds in his memory.

Another member who has also died was Martin Milligan. He had spent about three hours on the phone persuading me to stand as president, but it was Gordon that gave me the confidence to do the job and he really helped me. I can remember my first president's speech in Aberdeen, and as I sat down after delivering it Gordon put a gin and tonic in my hand and said, "Well done."

Gordon came with me to one of the biggest UK conferences in which I had to speak. It was a Civil Engineers' conference in September 1994, held at the St Nicholas Hotel, Scarborough, and it was attended by around 800 delegates. The Minister of Transport at the time was Roger Freeman, and it was usual practice for the Minister to speak first. However, for some reason that I cannot recall, I went first. It was at that conference dinner that I had red wine for the first time. We had roast beef and there was only red wine on the table, and I told Gordon I did not like it.

His response was, "Well, there's nothing else, so it's that or nothing." I did drink it and actually liked it, but would not admit that to Gordon. Ever since then that has been my favourite alcoholic drink, although I only have a little as I know it is good for me. Gordon had been a very fit person. He went rambling regularly and was always travelling up and down to London to attend meetings.

I was at a meeting in Athens when Gordon died. His wife had made him a cup of tea before going off to church, and when she got home she found him dead in his chair. I know for Gordon it was a lovely way to go, but for his family and friends it was a dreadful shock, and although it was 15 years ago I still miss him.

Two other members of the Environment Committee that became good friends of mine, and who have worked hard within the Federation, are Jack Tyrrell from Tyne and Wear and Hans Cohn, who lives in London. Hans, who is totally blind and also has a severe hearing problem, practised as a physiotherapist for many years. He edited the Federation's Viewpoint magazine for over 20 years, and at the age of 85 he still goes skiing.

It was just one year after Gordon's death that another very good friend to Alvin and me died suddenly. When I first went to live with Alvin there were two jobs that we needed help with. One was reading our post, as it was before Alvin had his corneal grafts, and the other was to pick up the dog mess from the garden. I asked at my church, expecting that a man would offer to help, but instead Daphne Imbush arrived, and she helped us with both these jobs for years, until her sudden death. She would also come twice a week with her dog to take me and my guide dog to the local woods, so the two dogs could have a free run together. Although one or two other people have done this too over the past few years, I really miss my twice-weekly long walk with Daphne. I knew Daphne from my days in the Girls' Brigade, as she was a nurse and had trained us for the home nursing and first aid awards that were presented to us at the Royal Albert Hall.

The contributions that these people have made, on both a professional and personal level, will never be forgotten.

CHAPTER 15 – RUBBING SHOULDERS WITH THE RICH AND FAMOUS

Throughout my life I have met so many famous people. It was only a few years after going blind that I met Cliff Richard, when he came to a local Christian house meeting, and I met many other stars when taking part in radio and television programmes, such as Esther Rantzen, Robert Kilroy Silk, Richard Littlejohn, Eric Morley and many Members of Parliament of all parties. I am also honoured to have made several visits to Buckingham Palace and met not only the Queen but also Lady Diana.

My first visit to Buckingham Palace was in 1978, the year of my father's death, when I attended a Duke of Edinburgh Award presentation. Gillian Anderson, one of the girls from my daughter's 1st Southend Girls' Brigade company, had helped me for a year with my reading, so when she went to receive her gold award she asked me to go with her as I was still an officer. As I'd had a lot of publicity about access for guide dogs in previous years, I contacted Douglas Kaye, who had written an article about me in the Woman's Own magazine. I knew he had worked at the Palace, so I asked him if he could find out whether I would be able to take Topsy into the Palace and he told me it would be fine. When we arrived at the Palace, as we were making our way to the cloakrooms, I was asked if I would like to keep Topsy with me or whether I would prefer to have someone to look after her and I chose to keep her with me. We were given a tour of the staterooms and picture gallery and then met the Duke, who presented the awards. Topsy was as good as usual and we had no trouble.

My second visit to the Palace was in 1981, the International Year of Disabled People, when 4,000 disabled people were invited to a garden party and I was given one of the ten tickets allocated to the Federation. A few days before the event I received a special invitation to have tea with the Queen in the royal tent. As I was going there on my own, I asked the director of Training for Guide Dogs, Derek Calver, to show me where to go at the set time. So he told his wife he would not be long and duly escorted me to the special tea tent. When we arrived they let Derek come in with me, which I really appreciated as I would not have known who was talking to me otherwise. A whole two hours passed before Derek returned to his wife, to be greeted by, "And where have you been?" "Just having tea with the Queen," was his reply.

In the tea tent there were 30 disabled people and 12 members of the royal family. It was just one week before Prince Charles and Lady Diana's wedding, so you can imagine how thrilled I was when Diana sat on the grass, chatting to me and stroking Topsy for ten minutes. Naturally she was upset to find out that I had gone blind on my wedding day.

The Queen spoke to me for about three minutes and asked me about my voluntary work, so I told her about our pavement campaign and the problems with access for guide dogs. I said we were still not allowed in the House of Commons and she thought that was very unfair. It was a wonderful day that I shall never forget, especially the chat with Lady Diana.

As important to me was the following day, when I went to speak at the morning assembly at Westborough School, close to where I live. I had gone to Sunday School with Shirley French, the headmistress of the school, and her mother, Mrs Cushings, had been an officer with my mum in the GLB. I attended in the dress and hat that I had worn at the Palace, and Topsy wore a bow made from my dress material. Lady Diana's perfume still lingered on Topsy's fur, and the children were so thrilled to smell it and hear all about my day at the Palace. It was their last day of term, and most of them were moving on to secondary school. It was certainly a very moving occasion for me.

It was less than two years later when I visited the Palace for the third time, but this time my guide dog was not allowed in. I was awarded an MBE in the New Year Honours list in 1983. When my invitation came to go to the Palace I was away at Leamington Spa, training with my third guide dog, Brandy, so one of the house ladies took me to the shops to help me choose a dress and jacket for the occasion. I can remember how thrilled the shop assistant was when she found out that my new outfit would be worn at the Palace. In order to match Brandy, who was a golden Labrador, I chose an apricot coloured dress and jacket, and once I got home I bought a chocolate brown hat, bag, gloves and shoes. It was all a bit of a rush, as I only arrived home from training on Friday 4th February and was due at the Palace on 10th February.

Mick and Jacqueline had gone with me, but once we arrived they were taken off somewhere else and Brandy was taken by a member of staff. I was then escorted to a special area, away from the other people who were awaiting their awards, where I met two other disabled people. I did not see any reason why Brandy could not have stayed with me. There was no food or drink, and we did not walk round the Palace as we had done on previous visits.

When I left, the Queen's private secretary brought Brandy back to me and said, "See you again one day, Mrs Allen." "What do you mean?" I said. "When you are made a Dame," he replied. "You must be joking!" I responded, as I was so cross that Brandy had been taken away from me. The press, who had been following my story, gave this matter a lot of publicity and it was raised in the House of Commons as well.

After leaving the Palace we went to Pimlico for a lunch that had been arranged by Sir Peter Baldwin, who had been permanent undersecretary of state at the Department of Transport and had chaired our committee at the Department for the past ten years. Ann Frye, head of the mobility unit at the Department of Transport, and Claudia Flanders, the widow of Michael Flanders, also came to the lunch. Although Sir Peter could not be there, he left me a bunch of freesias, which are my favourite flowers.

When I arrived home I was contacted to appear on breakfast television, and I was interviewed by Selina Scott the following morning on the live BBC Breakfast programme. Norman Hartnell, the Queen's dressmaker, was also a guest on the show, and he congratulated me on my outfit - that pleased me more than anything.

When I arrived home from London I received a call from Anglia Television, and they sent a taxi to pick me up and take me to Norwich for their Afternoon Live television show. My local paper, which had notified me about my award, also wrote a long feature about me.

On the day, the chairman of the National Bus Company arranged for a car to pick us up from home, and when we got to Victoria bus station we transferred to a chauffeur-driven car of his. I had heard that Brandy probably would not be allowed in, so I contacted Lord Snowdon and asked for his help. He assured me that everything would be fine, but when I arrived I was told that Brandy would not be allowed to stay with me. I just could not believe it. It seemed ironic that one of the reasons I was receiving the award was because of all the work I had done in regard to improving access for guide dogs, and also I had been there twice before with Topsy without any problem.

I will tell you about a most interesting person I encountered on one of my many long train journeys, when I was going to Liverpool to attend a conference. I had left home with my guide dog Lady and had travelled to Euston. It was a Monday morning and it was pouring with rain. On arrival at Euston a member of staff put me in a first-class compartment, as it was the nearest carriage, and also I think he felt sorry for me as I was dripping wet. When I took my seat there was only one other person in the carriage and he started talking to me straight away. He asked me all about Lady and the voluntary work I was doing.

It was about an hour into the journey before I asked him what he did. He had already told me he was going to Liverpool and would, therefore, help me to get off the train. He told me that he used to be a pop star but was now an artist and was going to an art exhibition. His name was Holly Johnson, from Frankie Goes to Hollywood.

Well, I must say that at the time I did not recognise his name, so when he exited the carriage to make a telephone call I too phoned Alvin and asked who he was. Alvin told me all about him and about his famous records, many of which he had in his shop. When I got to my hotel, I phoned my daughter to tell her. Normally Jacqueline is not really interested in all the people I meet, but on this occasion she was and she said she was very impressed.

Holly actually phoned me to make sure that I had got to my hotel okay. I told him that Jacqueline was very impressed that I had met him, and Holly said that he was very impressed to have met me as well. He was such a nice man and was so kind and helpful.

Joe Brown came into my life too, not only as someone that I loved to listen to in the sixties, but also because I discovered that Alvin had known Joe as a teenager. We met up with him in the late 1990s when he was appearing at the Cliffs Pavilion, Westcliff. We went backstage and he was so pleased to meet Alvin after all those years. He called Alvin 'Snowie', because he is an albino and had a lot of white hair when he was young.

When Joe found out about Alvin's music shop he asked him if he had an instrument called a primdomra. Alvin told him that they were Russian instruments, and it just so happened that I was going to Moscow the following June for one of my meetings. After visiting many shops in Moscow, I was able to buy Joe his instrument, and Alvin has now got a picture hanging in his shop of me handing it to Joe in his dressing room at the Cliffs Pavilion. Alvin and I like to go to the Cliffs when there are sixties music concerts, and we will often get up and dance in the aisle.

At a school function for the RNIB's Northwood School, where I was a governor, I met Rod Stewart. I told him about the sixties weekends that I organise each year, and he said he would like to come one day, but as yet he has not been able to do so. While talking to Rod, he asked me how I was getting home, so I told him I would be travelling on the underground, from Northwood station to Liverpool Street, and then on the main line train to Clacton and would then take a taxi to my bungalow. He actually offered to pay for a taxi to take me all the way, but I did not take up his offer.

I think some of the people I meet do remember me for different reasons. One of the Ministers of Transport was Steven Norris. I had taken him for a walk round the Westminster block of streets, pointing out all the hazards on the pavements. On the occasions that I have met him since then, he says he always thinks about me when he does that walk. I tell him that he should get rid of all those hazardous bollards, not just look at them! Many other people have said that they always think of me when they park on the pavement, and I have to remind them that it is illegal and what a hazard they are causing.

For many years we used to go camping at Lowestoft, and there was a little theatre there where we met Leslie Crowther a few times. Another television personality I met, when we made Get Streetwise, was Tony Robinson, who is featured in the video. And I also met another member of the royal family, Princess Margaret, when I was in the finals of the Woman of the Year competition.

While it has been nice to meet some of these celebrities, I have enjoyed meeting so many different people on my travels throughout the UK and in other countries.

Although I like to talk a lot, over the years I have learnt to listen to other people and to their different views on issues, even if I do not always agree with them. However, there are two issues that have affected my life and that I will always speak out about: measles and smoking.

Measles was the cause of my blindness, and I just cannot understand why parents still refuse to have their children vaccinated against this dangerous disease. Before the vaccination was introduced, so many children suffered with sight impairment and other disabilities and, of course, many died.

As for smoking, if I had known the impact that smoking could have on people's lives I would never have worked as a directors' cook for Gallaher's. Although they paid me for a year after I went blind, until Jacqueline was born (and without that money we probably would have had to give up our house), if I had known the dramatic effect that the death of my best friend and neighbour, Pam, from smoking-related cancer would have on me, and on her loving husband and three young children, I would never have worked for them.

My first husband, Mick, had asthma, and contact with smokers at our home or when out and about would always trigger an asthma attack. I have never had a cigarette in my life. When I was young one or two of my friends started to smoke, but most of us just could not afford it. In the catering profession we were not allowed to smoke, which probably helped us from getting this dreadful habit.

Because I have a very sensitive nose, I hate the smell of smoke. I particularly dislike it when my clothes stink of smoke after I have been somewhere where people have been smoking, and I immediately have to take them off and wash them all. We will not let anyone smoke in our house and for years we have displayed 'no smoking' notices. I am pleased to say that most of our friends do not smoke.

EPILOGUE

It is now 11th November 2009, Remembrance Day, and I am in Majorca with Alvin and guide dog Amanda for our annual two-weeks holiday.

This is a fitting date for the completion of my book, as it holds very special significance for me. It was the birth date of the grandma I never knew, Miriam Clarke, and it was also the day I qualified with my first guide dog, Topsy, back in 1971 at Leamington Spa Training Centre.

Looking back over the past 69 years, despite going blind and having to struggle for many years with very little money, I have had a happy life and many moving experiences. I think I managed very well with sight in just one eye, and if I had received more help and proper rehabilitation I could have coped a lot better with my total blindness.

Being totally blind is so different from having even a little vision. I naturally wish I could see my daughter and my two grandchildren, Emily and Joseph. But when I think of my friends Moira, Lily, Barbara and Cynthia, who have all lost their husbands and have no children or grandchildren, I think I am lucky to have a wonderful daughter and son-in-law and two lovely grandchildren.

I also think of my friend Peter, who has helped me to complete this book and who has been totally blind since birth. At least I can remember what the sky, the sun, the moon and the stars look like. The sight of a rainbow I shall never forget. It made me appreciate the sight I had once had when Peter was sitting in my kitchen one day, while I was preparing food for one of my parties, and learnt that he had never seen or felt a whole cucumber, parsnip and some other food items.

When I went totally blind, I did think: why should God do this to me? And when Jacqueline was eight she asked me why she should say her prayers when God would not let me see. Well, of course, I still sometimes wonder why, but then I ponder on the fact that without my blindness and the experiences I went through I could not have helped other people.

A hundred people go blind every day in the UK, and I am sure many of those people will think it is the end of the world. However, as I have found out, you can still have a fulfilling life. Yes, it will be different and will require lots of adjusting, but with the help of your friends and family you will cope, just as I have done.

If only everyone had their eyes tested regularly and took the treatment they were given, the sight of so many more people could be saved. Sight is something we tend to take for granted; I did, until I went totally blind.

As I approach my seventieth birthday, I am still fit enough to go out each day for walks with my husband and my guide dog, to attend meetings at home and abroad, and to enjoy time with my friends and family.

I will continue to campaign to improve the quality of life for all blind people, by whatever means I can.

Left:Me with my father, 1943

Below: Me, aged 6, 1946

Above: Me with Barbara Windsor
and Topsy, Southend, 1975

Right: Me, Mick and Jacqueline, first prize
winners at the Southend carnival, 1968

Below: My wedding photo, 1964

LIVELY LADY

Jacqueline Allen, my daughter, this photo was in the local paper, 1969

Me with my first guide dog, Topsy, 1971

Above left: Me and Bunty, my second guide dog, which I had for only 6 months, 1982

Above right: Me, Mick, Jacqueline and Brandy, at the Palace with my MBE, 1983

Left: My wedding with Alvin with Quella Otis and Mum, 1987

Left: Speaking at the Liberal
Party Conference, 1987

Below: Me, Joseph and Emily
on my 60th birthday, 2000

Above: Me with Joe Brown, Southend, June 2003

Above: Talking to a class of children
with Brandy, one of my 800 talks! 1984

Right: At the Radcliff Awards, with
Ann Frye and Jean Radcliff, 1992

Left: Finalist at the 'Woman of the Year' awards, with chairman, 1992

Below: Me talking with Thena Heshell, 1992

Me with 'Lady' and the deputy mayor Norman Harris at the N.F.B. conference, Eastbourne, 2002

Talking with the Prime Minister John Major, 1993

Me, Alvin and Amanda at the Mayor's ball, Southend, with Brian and Linda Smith, May 2009

Right: Me and Amanda with the brownies at Chalkwell Methodist Church, December 2009

www.apexpublishing.co.uk

Lightning Source UK Ltd.
Milton Keynes UK
UKHW040616281018
331340UK00001B/27/P